Endorsements

This book takes you almost everywhere. To Hippo Hole where large beasts snort and babies dive off their mothers' backs and to the floor of a hostel during a military coup while bombs fall from the sky and machine guns rattle outside. You'll eat *injera* in Ethiopia, *ugali* in Kenya, *lahmacun* in Turkey, peaches in Virginia, and Lebanon baloney in Lancaster, Pennsylvania. You'll beat trees with broom sticks until green and black olives rain down on you. And you'll be evicted from a country. As you read, you'll feel strangeness wash over you, again and again. And with Jewel, you'll share the aching for home that lives in all of us. *Finding Home* will help you understand not only its author, but also yourself and your longing for a place to belong.

—Phyllis Swartz, author of *Yoder School*, teacher for 35 years, educational consultant, blogger at Apple to Apple

As president of Rosedale Bible College, I recognize our students' hunger for security, rootedness, and belonging. Jewel Showalter's *Finding Home* is the story they need. Unpretentious and sincere, the book reveals God's work in a lifetime of cross-cultural endeavors, showing a new generation that home is not a place, but rootedness in God.

—Jeremy Miller, President, Rosedale Bible College

Jewel Showalter's *Finding Home* is a vital, compelling account of a life lived without borders. Raised in pioneering Ethiopia and later serving alongside her late husband, EMM's 6th President, Richard Showalter, Jewel's story chronicles the transformative results of mid-20th-century Mennonite missions—a legacy that includes the world's largest Anabaptist body, the Meserete Kristos Church. This memoir offers essential historical documentation while powerfully exploring the universal search for belonging, where physical geography never becomes a spiritual destiny. A necessary read on faith, legacy, and the true meaning of home.

—Marvin Lorenzana, President, Eastern Mennonite Missions

Finding Home is a beautifully told story of life lived to the full, learning to follow Jesus. Jewel's honest and vulnerable reflections caused me to laugh out loud and moved me to tears. *Finding Home* will call us all to reflect more deeply on how we respond to His voice when asked to trust more, to go further, to worship wholeheartedly, and to forgive completely. Thanks Jewel!

—Darren Peachey, Conference Pastor, Rosedale Network of Churches

Whether Jewel describes a California-style hippie bandana or a rumpled Lancaster Mennonite headcovering; a thermos of goldenrod tea or a full-page ad for Johnnie Walker whiskey; Miss Havisham's yellowing wedding dress, or the white, clean linens of the Bride of Christ—her story sings, often literally, of God's great faithfulness to His people, throughout all seasons. Jewel's memoirs are all the more potent for me and my house, because we are the direct beneficiaries of her passion for the "inclusion of the Gentiles" in the Showalter's native tribe. These are stories to read, and to read with your children, and to read with your children's children. By preserving these memories for future generations, Jewel has done a great service, not only for her own immediate family but also for God's entire household, adopted in Christ.

—Matthew Cordella, Pastor of Pike Mennonite Church in Elida, Ohio, father of four, and a visiting faculty member at Rosedale Bible College

Finding Home is a rare look inside the heart and mind of one who has experienced the length, depth, and breadth of a lifetime of mission. Here you'll find wonder and adventure, danger and risk, joy and suffering—all part of the call of Jesus to go anywhere and everywhere with the beautiful news that His kingdom is here. You can't miss the obvious conclusion that in that call is where, generation after generation, we all find home.

—Joe Showalter has been president of Rosedale International (formerly Rosedale Mennonite Missions) for 24 years. He and his wife Janice founded and lead the Columbus Network of Microchurches.

We hear the expression of a "Favorite Son" of some particular locality so perhaps we, of the Mt. Pleasant Mennonite community would do well to consider Jewel our "Favorite Daughter." Who could have known that God had His hand on the little girl we went to school with, to use her in so many ways, in so many places around the world, to speak His name to those who needed to hear it? *Finding Home* is a candid, behind-the-scenes glimpse of the personal cost/loss incurred when we respond to God's call on our lives for His Glory. Today we may weep but tomorrow we shall rejoice.

—Dale Keffer is a retired pastor and renewal speaker from Chesapeake, Virginia. He serves as an overseer for ten churches, most within the Rosedale Network of Churches.

I enjoyed reading *Finding Home* immensely. After all, it's written by my sister and overlaps a bit with childhood memories. On one level, Jewel has written a memoir packed with adventure. But on a deeper level, she recounts a personal spiritual pilgrimage of finding home with God, with strangers, neighbors, and with herself through the twists and turns of a life often lived literally on the road.

—Mark R. Wenger is a retired pastor and seminary educator. He serves as a bishop/overseer in the LanChester District of LMC.

If you've ever wondered what life as a missionary is like, join Jewel in her new book, *Finding Home*. In an honest, easy-flowing manner, she shares the challenges, joys, struggles, and questions on God's path for her as a woman, wife, mother, friend, and follower of Jesus.

—Peggy Duffy, a retired school teacher with 30 years of experience, a friend and hiking partner

Having navigated the unpredictable nature of the foster care system after losing my mother at a young age, a stable, secure "home" has always felt elusive and perpetually out of reach. Jewel's experience of searching for a fixed emotional anchor beautifully mirrors the spiritual instability many of us feel when we try to steer our own way. Her powerful message—that no matter where the adventure takes us or how uncertain the future looks, we are at rest and truly at home with Jesus—finally made that unreachable concept real. This book is a profound and comforting reminder that the best and safest place to rest is always in His presence.

—Paula J. Ryan, a friend and fellow pilgrim

FINDING HOME

Finding Home

A Memoir

Jewel Showalter

SANTOS BOOKS

EVERY STORY SACRED

First Printing, 2025

Published by Santos Books LLC, Elizabethtown, PA 17022

Conrad L. Kanagy, Executive Publisher and CEO

ISBN: 979-8-9994186-9-2

Contents

Acknowledgments   xii

Preface   xv

Foreword   xix

Part I   1

  1 Peach Country   3

  2 Pioneering Days in Ethiopia   17

  3 The First Five Years   27

  4 Bingham Academy   39

  5 An Ever-present Father   53

  6 Fitting In   61

  7 Things Get Worse   67

  8 Good Shepherd School   73

  9 Never Say Never   83

10 Goodbye Ethiopia. Hello America   91

11 Alone with the Mennonites   105

Part 2   113

12 Off to College   115

13 First Real Jobs   133

14 Off to California   147

15 A Home in Rosedale   159

16 Off to Kenya and Turkey   175

17 Gaziantep and the Southeast   193

18 Turkish Republic of North Cyprus   213

19 Rosedale Bible College   227

20 Lancaster, Pennsylvania   235

21 Global South Partnerships   251

22 Epilogue   263

About the Author   267
Appendices   269
Glossary   293

To my children and their spouses, my grandchildren, and their children for a thousand generations. May you always find a home in the Lord who has been "our dwelling place through all generations."

Acknowledgments

My sincere thanks to my three beloved children, Chad, Rhoda, and Matthew, who lived many of these stories with me and who continue to support and encourage me in every way imaginable, even after all I dragged them through! Their spouses, Deborah, Keith, and Colleen, are also deeply loved and helpful in countless ways, including practical things like photos, meals, and editorial comments. I also want to acknowledge my late husband Richard, whose sensitive, undying love encouraged me to grow in a faith that stretched my more settled preferences with his irresistible pioneering visions.

Preface

"When an old person dies, the library burns," says the old African proverb. My children always begged for stories, and now my grandchildren. So before my library burns, I want to leave this record of my life. Sometimes the events seem almost fantastical. Did all these things really happen? Have I been too simplistic, too Pollyannaish, too matter of fact, too embellishing? Memory is flawed. Perspective is limited. But I have seen the face of God. I feel like the richest old lady in the world. As you enter my story and write your own, you too can gain riches eternal.

Ever since I can remember I've felt like a misfit, an outsider. Maybe everyone does? For me it started in 1949 when I was only one year old. My parents moved me from southern Virginia to Ethiopia. Part of a Mennonite mission team. Since then, I've hopscotched schools, churches, and countries. As an adult too. At 20 I married an inveterate missionary explorer, and we made homes on three continents. I quickly feel at home almost anywhere, but then not really quite at home. Not like those "rooted" Mennonites who say, "My mother carried me into this church when I was born, and they'll carry me out when my time comes."

Not many of us know that kind of rootedness anymore. Not even Mennonites. But we all long for a place to belong, a home. We want to know we're part of a community, a "tribe."

And what does God have to do with all of this? Do we find ourselves "rich in things but poor in soul," as the old hymn says? There's a growing loneliness, anxiety, and depression creeping ever wider among us.

In these pages I invite you into the story of what for me has been the secret of feeling at home anywhere. I share these shaping stories and memories with the hope that wherever you have been born and wherever you have wandered you can also know Home.

"Lord, you have been our dwelling place through all generations. Before the mountains were born or you brought forth the earth and the sea. From everlasting to everlasting, you are God." Ps. 90:1.

Foreword

Jewel Showalter's *Finding Home* is more than a story. It is a profound and transformative record of a life wholly devoted to serving others. As I was reading, I found myself thinking, "This feels like the next chapter of the book of Acts." This book graciously unveils the hidden sacrifices and victories of ministry, offering readers an intimate look into Jewel's family and the deep costs of serving in God's kingdom.

Having been personally mentored by Jewel and Richard in both mission work and family life, including my daughters Meklit and Tsega, I have witnessed the cost of life poured out for others. Also for the Meserete Kristos Church (MKC), Jewel's family has been an enduring blessing for three generations. Their legacy is a powerful reminder that true blessing is born from courage, dedication, and perseverance through suffering.

Jewel's story unveils a profound spiritual truth: to be a blessing to others, someone must suffer. Her life and legacy bear witness to this reality. Beginning her mission journey at one year of age in Ethiopia and continuing through decades of cross-cultural ministry in places like Kenya, Turkey, the Middle East, Latin America, Asia and Europe. Jewel has faced painful loss, continual transitions, and costly sacrifices.

Yet, her willingness to surrender has yielded remarkable fruit, both in her own life and in the lives of countless others. Her writing radiates this depth and invites readers to embrace the same transformative path. In this book, she invites us to explore places where pain and purpose meet. Her reflections on grief, obedience, and belonging are not abstract; they are revealed, explained, and lived. Through it all, she points to the faithfulness of God, who meets us in every season and calls us to be vessels of His blessing.

This book is a gift to all who serve, especially those navigating the tension between calling and cost. For us, MKC members, it is a mirror and a mantle, reminding us of the legacy we carry and the grace that sustains us. It is no coincidence that Meserete Kristos Church is now the largest Mennonite church in the world. That growth is rooted in the obedience and sacrifice of pioneers like Jewel's family, whose lives continue to bear fruit throughout generations.

Yemiru T. Mintesenot, Ph.D.
Former Meserete Kristos Church Mission Director
Africa Mission Partnership Initiative Director
Immigrant Church Growth Consultant for Rosedale International

Part I

1

Peach Country

We were walking up the long farm lane, Papa and me. It was a quarter mile to the mailbox, past peach trees pushing pink in early spring. The air was cool, and I bounced along, trying to miss the dark mud oozing soil on my new white sneakers.

My eighth birthday was coming up, and I knew what would happen. We'd go back to Ethiopia. Papa said we first went there when I was just a year old on a big ocean freighter. So, of course, I don't remember that trip. But Papa said Grandma Weaver, who saw us off at the dock, was scared I'd fall through the wide pipe rails edging the deck of the ship. She rushed out and bought a baby harness.

"I never used that harness," Papa told me with a snort. "A leash to keep my girls in check? Did she think I couldn't control my own children?" We were safe when Papa was around.

From Wenger family prayer card.

Papa said there'd been busloads of people that came to New York to see us off. People they'd gone to college with, friends like David and Rhoda Showalter, folks from our home church, Mount Pleasant Mennonite in Fentress, Virginia, and relatives like Grandpa and Grandma Weaver. Mama gave all these people tours of the ship and our below-deck cabins with round porthole windows.

Before all our friends left, they gathered around us and sang: *"God be with you 'til we meet again; By His counsel guide you. With His sheep securely fold you. God be with you 'til we meet again."*

And then that trilling chorus up and away, *"Til we me-ee-eet , 'til we me-et, 'til we meet at Jesus feet,"* with the men's bass adding, *"til we meet."* And everyone taking up, *"God be with you 'til we meet again."*

People wiped tears from their eyes. We were going away for five years. To Africa. Would there ever be a meeting here on earth?

There was a second song we always sang at times like this. *"Blest be the tie that binds our hearts in Christian love, the fellowship of kindred minds is like to that above."*

The second verse isn't so sweet. All through my childhood it conjured violent images in my mind, *"When we asunder part, it gives us inward pain."* (I'd imagine being torn limb from limb and snicker with my friends to stop the pushing tears.) *"But we shall still be joined in heart and hope to meet again."*

These were our leaving songs. I get knots in my stomach just thinking about it. *"The tie that binds our hearts in Christian love..."* It's strong and stretchy. It squeezes. Sometimes it snaps back and stings you like a wet tea towel when you have to dry dishes with your brother. Sometimes it breaks. But it keeps you from falling. Usually.

It was a month-long voyage across the Atlantic in hurricane season, past the Straits of Gibraltar, through the Mediterranean Sea, the Suez Canal and Red Sea to Djibouti in the horn of Africa.

Freighter that took the Wenger family to Ethiopia.

Papa said the sea was so rough our suitcases and trunks under the beds crashed from side to side as the ship rocked. One minute we'd see water through our little portholes, then the next minute we'd see sky. To keep my highchair anchored Papa hooked his long legs through the rungs. And the tables had ledges you flipped up to keep the dishes from scooting off.

I didn't remember any of that, but it seemed like I did. I'd heard it so many times. But here I was, seven years old, and it was time to go back to Ethiopia—again. And I knew what would happen this time. Something worse than a hurricane at sea. I'd have to go away to a boarding school for missionary children. I looked up at Papa to see if there might be some escape.

"Do I have to go away to boarding school? Can't Mama teach me at home like before?" I begged.

Papa looked straight ahead, not meeting my eyes as I skipped along dodging puddles in the muddy farm lane. "Jewel, I wish there was another way. We don't like sending you children away, but that's the mission policy."

We reached our two-story white frame farmhouse. Papa took the mail inside, but I ran to my crepe myrtle tree beside the old shed. The vivid magenta blossoms created a lacy shade. I climbed the spreading branches to a seat where I braced my elbows on another branch that I played like Mama's organ. Then the branch became a typewriter. I pecked out papers for Papa's seminary classes like Mama did to help him.

Dusk dulled the pink peach blossoms and turned on the lights. I loved our family, this little farm. Why did I have to leave? Go someplace far away. Where I didn't know anybody. And without my family. With my family I'd be like a turtle—carry my house around with me. So it wouldn't be that hard changing houses. But leaving Papa and Mama? Going to boarding school?

I looked up to the heavens. There was the evening star, Venus, Papa called it. I started humming, *"There's a city of light 'mid the stars, we are told; where they know not a sorrow or care..."*

Papa said someday Jesus would come back and take us all to heaven, that city up in the stars. The good people that is. It could happen any day. Maybe Jesus would come back before boarding school. Maybe I'd be whisked away, escape it all. I sure hoped so. Maybe I wouldn't have to go to boarding school after all.

We'd lived on this little farm for two years now, a furlough from work in Ethiopia so Papa could get more education. Mama said this is where she and Papa lived before they got married. It's the house where I was born. "Back to our roots," Papa always said.

During those past two years we'd loved playing under the grape arbor and swinging on the long rope swing knotted high up in the silvery beech behind the house. Every day we'd walked about a quarter mile to the little two-room schoolhouse, Mt. Pleasant Christian Day School. Aunt Lenora, married to Papa's oldest brother Amos, taught grades 1-6. Uncle Amos taught grades 7-10.

The old farm house in peach country.

In Ethiopia those first five years, Mama had taught us at home. She didn't send us away to boarding school like she was supposed to. But she knew she couldn't hold out forever. Maybe if I cried hard enough, she'd change her mind, stand up to the mission.

She'd taught my sister Betty grades one to three and Margaret grade one. I got grade one too, without even trying. Mama said that when she taught the older girls at the dining room table, I'd always do everything Margaret did. "Second-to-None!" Mama called me. "Always trying to keep up with your older sisters, are you?" That's how I skipped a year ahead—and people thought Margaret and I were twins. But she was really 14 months older.

School in America was fun too, especially reading. Aunt Lenora had us sit up front on little chairs and read out loud while the other students worked quietly at their desks. At recess we could play with the older kids too. One day there was a kite flying contest to see whose kite would go the highest. Uncle Amos was the judge. Of course, one of the big boys won. I didn't know how to fly a kite. We never had them in Ethiopia. Mine just went around in circles and hit the ground. Maybe it needed a tail or something. So many new things to learn. I wasn't going to get left behind.

But the swings. I loved them. Long ropes from a tall oak. Three side by side. We'd go front, back and sideways, fighting to knock into each other, to bump each other off. "Dog fights," we called them.

I was good in school because I didn't want to get sent to the principal even if he was my uncle. Uncle Amos had the sharpest blue eyes you ever did see. All the children said he could look right through you—and I believed it.

Uncle Amos and Aunt Lenora lived on the farm beside us and took care of the peach orchards and the vineyards. Part of it belonged to us, but since we were in Ethiopia most of the time, they took care of our land too.

That winter it snowed. It doesn't usually snow much in southern Virginia, but Mama said it was a "gift from God" for her 'African' children who had never seen snow. Cousin Jamie pulled us on sleds behind the tractor, trying to throw us off as he spun in big circles. I clung on to Margaret, but then we both fell off rolling in the dusty cold crystals. I stuck out my tongue. It was just water. Not even sweet like ice-cream.

As the snow melted away and the weather warmed, Papa said he hoped it didn't get warm too fast. If there was an early spring—and the peach trees bloomed—and then there was another freeze—the peach crop would be ruined.

The air smelled of burning rubber. Papa said Uncle Amos and Cousin Jamie had been up all night checking the temperatures and lighting stacks of old rubber tires, throwing up a smoke screen to save the peach blooms from freezing.

At breakfast Papa sang a song he'd learned from his mama, Annie (Lehman) Wenger who moved here from Pennsylvania with my grandpa A.D. Wenger. They're the ones who planted the first peach trees and vineyards on this land. They also started the church and school.

"Little cherry blossom lived up in a tree
And a very happy little thing was she
Clad all through the winter in her coat of brown
For she was a-living in a northern town.

Then one sunny morning, thinking it was May
"I'll not wear," said blossom, "this old coat today."
Do be careful blossom, winter has not fled
And Jack Frost may nip you in your cozy bed.

Blossom would not listen for the sky was bright
And she wished to glisten in her robe of white
So she let the brown one drop and blow away
Leaving her the white one all so fine and gay.

Bye and bye the sunshine faded from her view
How poor blossom shivered as it colder grew
Oh, for that warm wrapper lying on the ground
Now Jack Frost will nip; he is prowling round

Ah, poor cherry blossom, she in foolish pride
Changed her proper clothing, took a cold and died.
All you little blossoms, hear me and take care;
Go not clad too lightly and of pride beware.

We picked up the jingle—substituting "peachy" for "cherry" and sang it all the way across the fields as we walked to school that day hoping that the blossoms would heed our warning and not pop out of their brown bud coats. Papa told us the smoky fires saved most of the peaches. A few weeks later the orchard burst out in pink, and that summer we ate all the peaches we wanted.

In Ethiopia we ate papayas, bananas, oranges, and guavas. But this was the first I'd tasted peaches and apples. Maybe we should stay here in peach country and never go back to Ethiopia and boarding school. Maybe this was a good place "to put down roots" like Grandpa and Grandma.

Now that I could read, Papa and Mama gave me my first Bible. It had a black leather cover and thin onion skin paper pages with gold edging. I was proud of my Bible and carried it to church every Sunday. In Sunday School class we memorized Bible verses, and I loved earning the blue and red prize cards for memorization.

I liked church. Not like Ethiopia where the preacher spoke Amharic. One Sunday a tall man called George Brunk came. I felt close to God. Each night we sang, *"Just as I am without one plea..."* The song made me cry. *"Oh, Lamb of God, I come, I come."* People went front to pray with Brother Brunk. I came too, safe, part of the group. If they were all going to heaven, I wanted to go, too.

I wrote a special verse I memorized in the front of my Bible. John 3:16. God really did love the whole world, it said. And then the rest of the chapter talked about the wind—God's Spirit was like the wind, blowing wherever it wanted. We didn't know where it came from or where it went.

I liked to read by myself, but mostly I liked when Mama read to us and it was my turn to sit beside her, to press against her soft leg and lean in to see the pictures. Mama read all kinds of stories and poetry.

"Who has seen the wind?
Neither you nor I.
But when the leaves hang trembling
The wind is passing by.
Who has seen the wind?
Neither I nor you.
But when the trees bow down their heads,
The wind is passing through."

"The wind is passing by, the wind is passing through..." I chanted the words to myself as I tried to go to sleep. Then a strong gust of wind blew open the bedroom door.

"What's that," Margaret sat up, her fearful brown eyes scanning the room.

"It's just the wind," I said. "Mr. Wind, Mr. Wind, why did you open our door and peak in?"

"You made up a poem!" Margaret said. We giggled and snuggled down to sleep.

I liked the wind. Usually. When we came back here to peach country on that big ocean freighter, the wind blew my braids out like flags and flung sea water in my face as I raced around the decks. It was scary strong.

Where did it come from? I knew that Bible story about the little fishing boat that got caught in a storm. When it was almost ready to sink Jesus made the wind stop. And it did. Everyone was amazed. No one can control the wind—except Jesus. Ships sink and houses fall down just because of the wind.

Then we heard that Hurricane Hazel was headed to hit peach country on the Virginia coast. I didn't know what a hurricane was, but Uncle Amos said the winds were so strong we shouldn't stay in our old farmhouse. The big beech tree might split and come down right on top of us. Cousin John and his wife Edith invited us to spend the night with them. They had a strong brick house. More secure.

The winds picked up as we packed overnight bags. The porch screen door slammed, and I looked back at the beech tree waving its huge branches over the house. Our swing ropes jerked crazily. Would I ever see the house again? Could Jesus stop this wind?

Cousin Edith spread quilts and comforters on her living room floor. We slept makeshift. The next morning, we drove home along roads littered with branches and storm debris. Was our house still standing? It was!

Uncle Amos told us he'd been up in the middle of the night working to save the chicken house. He staked it with strong ropes to keep it from blowing off the foundations.

"The long building rippled like a snake," he said. "But I was able to save the chickens."

Papa just shook his head. "Amos, that was dangerous. Sure you want to risk your life for some chickens?"

Uncle Amos smiled with those piercing blue eyes. "Chester, you'd have done the same thing if they were your chickens."

I climbed into my crepe myrtle tree. It was still standing. Small but tough. All around tall pines lay uprooted like so many horse weeds in a bean field. And the old shed by the house had collapsed like a stack of blocks. But nothing touched my tree. It would bend but never break. I slid down a long supple branch. It bounded back like a spring as I ran inside. The wind couldn't hurt it.

Wenger family waiting to board ship.

2

Pioneering Days in Ethiopia

Exploring the grounds of Dedar in front of our first home.

I liked when Mama told me stories from those early times in Ethiopia, those days before we came back here to peach country. Sometimes I thought I almost remembered—like one of the first evenings soon after we'd arrived at our first home in the highlands of Dedar.

At bedtime Mama found us three little girls covered with ticks. We'd spent the afternoon clamoring over the wood pile. Building tiny teeter totters and teepees for our dolls, crafting cups and saucers from eucalyptus acorns.

She yelled for Papa, who came running into the circle of light thrown from the one bulb powered by a generator. The missionary nurse with us said those ticks carried a deadly fever, and they'd have to bathe us immediately. Papa grabbed two buckets and ran for the mountain spring. Mama stirred up embers from the cooking fire and added wood—all the while combing through our long brown hair and undressing us, searching for ticks.

When Papa returned from the spring, he dumped the water into a big black pot balanced on stones over the fire. Mama unfolded a gray canvas tub near the fire. It took too long for the cold spring water to heat, but as soon as little wisps of steam swirled up from the pot Papa poured the water into the canvas tub. In we went, all three of us at once, lathered good.

Warning us not to play in the wood pile again, Papa slung a rope swing from the branches of a giant eucalyptus near the garage. My older sisters loved to mother me. "Jewel, come here. Jewel, let me push you on the swing. Here Jewel, look at the donkeys."

We were living in a little cinder block garage, the first building on a compound that would expand to include an elementary school and a hospital. I was too young to know or care about all that. I toddled around, trying to keep up with my older sisters. That's when they first started calling me "Second-to-None."

Curious Oromo children peeked at us from behind trees and huts. They'd never seen white people before. They were filled with questions about how we lived and why we'd come, but we didn't understand each other's languages. The only school in these parts was run by the priests at the Coptic Orthodox Church who gathered clusters of young lads around them to chant the Amharic alphabet.

Then Mama noticed something funny. A group of boys from the village had grown bolder. They squatted in the grass nearby watching us play. Every time my sisters called out, "Jewel" the boys burst out laughing and yelled back, "Joedlee, Joedlee"—pointing to me.

Papa decided to investigate. He'd been picking up a bit of language as he worked with local men hired to help with construction. From them he learned that the Oromo word for baby was "Joedlee". When the children heard my sisters calling "Jewel, Jewel" it sounded to them like my sisters were calling, "Baby, Baby." I was, of course, the baby. Our worlds were totally different, but we had at least one word in common.

Mama and Papa had hoped to stay in Dedar, but that little cinderblock home Papa built went to another family, and we were whisked away to Nazareth, a larger city on the escarpment south of the capital city Addis Ababa.

The Mennonite mission director, Orie O. Miller, had paid a visit. We were all new to the task of missions in Ethiopia—Orie and the group of committed young adults he'd led to desert their bucolic Pennsylvania and Virginia farms to confront the world's needs.

Ethiopia was just recovering from a war, and the returning Emperor Haile Selassie welcomed mission groups with open arms. He needed schools and hospitals. Ethiopia was officially a Christian country. Little, round Coptic churches dotted the surrounding hilltops. The emperor wanted mission groups to work especially in the Muslim and animistic regions of the country.

Nazareth was a mixed region but predominantly Coptic Christian. The emperor invited the Mennonites to establish a hospital there, in an old cotton gin, but not to baptize and start new churches. Ethiopia already had a church, an ancient one. They didn't need "a new religion that came over on a ship" and one that "hated the Virgin Mary." They'd already been Christians for more than a thousand years.

Our first home in Nazareth. Jewel is riding in an improvised bike seat created by a diaper slung between Mama's handlebars.

So moving to Nazareth was the right thing to do. Orie said so, and when Orie spoke, things happened. Orie said Nazareth was a good place to learn Amharic, the language the emperor hoped could unify his mountainous empire with its hundreds of tribal groups and languages. Papa had already learned some Oromo but now he tackled Amharic.

Typical Coptic Orthodox church.

From our home on the hospital compound, we could see a Coptic church perched on the mountains to the north, but we believed the whole country was really non-Christian—compared to America that is. No one read the Bible. They knew it was a holy book and loved to kiss it. But only the priests with their long gray beards and flowing tunics chanted the scriptures in Geez, an ancient form of Amharic that no one really understood anymore.

One day a priest came on to the hospital compound to greet Papa. He extended a large silver cross for Papa to kiss. Papa greeted him warmly but didn't kiss the cross like the other Ethiopians.

"Why don't you kiss the cross?" I asked Papa.

"The priest thinks that kissing the cross or the Bible will save the people," Papa said. "But we believe that Jesus died to save us from our sins. We don't need to be kissing crosses and giving money to the priest to earn our salvation. We want to teach the people what's actually in their holy book—after they kiss it.

"Oh," I said. "Does the priest know that?"

Not only Coptic priests came to visit, but hundreds of sick people walked or rode in horse drawn carts, *garys,* to the hospital the mission started. They sat on the grass waiting to see the doctor. I watched them come in the lane that ran right by my favorite tree—crippled people limping, blind people led by friends, tiny children slung on mothers' backs.

Each day I climbed my tree—a flat-topped bean tree with knobby pods that grew beside the hospital lane. I watched the sick people come—some so weak their friends carted them in wheel barrows or *garys.*

People with elephantiasis especially frightened me. They walked slowly dragging along their huge legs—so swollen and painful they looked like elephant's legs. What made them that way? Could the doctors help them? Might my legs get that way too? Each day before I climbed to my perch in the tree, I examined my legs to make sure they were both still the same size.

And the blind people, the lepers with deformed hands, feet, and faces. Mama said leprosy killed your nerves so you couldn't feel anything. That might seem good sometimes, like when you step on a big thorn. But Mama said that pain is actually a good thing. It tells you something is wrong so you can fix it. If you never felt the thorn prick or the burn from the cooking fire—or the blister from too much hiking, the sore place would get infected and could ruin your whole foot!

That's why I'd see lepers with only stubs of fingers or sometimes without any toes. One had no nose, just two holes in his face. He scared me so much I ran away and stubbed my toe bad on the edge of the cement porch. I cried out in pain, then rubbed away the tears. That proved I didn't have leprosy!

One day at breakfast Mama said sharply, "Jewel, don't let flies sit on your eyes. Flies carry trachoma. If they sit on the eyes of a person with trachoma and then sit on your eyes, your eyes could become infected too."

I swung at the fly. He'd just left my face and moved to the jam jar. Had he just sat on the eyes of one of the hospital patients? Mama said that trachoma made your eye lashes turn in so they scratched your eyeballs every time you blinked, and slowly but surely, you'd go blind with all that scraping. My lashes seemed soft enough, but what if they started turning in? Each morning, I examined my eyes in the mirror.

But what about the blind people and the lepers? Could our hospital heal them? Jesus healed blind people and lepers. Then my older sister Betty got an idea. While people waited to see the doctor, we could tell them Bible stories about Jesus, how he healed the blind and made the lame people walk.

Since we couldn't speak much Amharic yet, Betty told Bible stories in English and one of the nursing students interpreted into Amharic. I was so proud to see everyone listening to the stories. Now I felt like I was helping people too. Could Jesus heal their bodies and their hearts? I sure hoped so. The stories we told were in their holy book, but they'd never heard them before.

We sang little choruses we knew too—"Jesus Loves Me" and "Heavenly Sunshine." Our Ethiopian friends quickly translated them into Amharic. The tunes were different from Ethiopian music—strange, but fun.

But then I got sick. Not elephantiasis or trachoma, but malaria. That comes from mosquitoes. The female ones that stick their hind ends up in the air. They're the carriers. They bite someone with malaria and then they bite you. That's how it spreads.

Each night before we went to bed Mama checked on the walls beside our beds for mosquitoes. She stalked around with a swatter. Mosquitoes bite at night. Sometimes we slept under nets, but since Nazareth was dry there weren't many mosquitoes. We thought we didn't need nets. But I still got malaria. Maybe it happened in Dedar.

I got so hot I threw off all my covers. I tried to take off my PJ's too. "Bring me a drink of water," I cried. "Water. Water. I'm burning up." The next minute I was so cold my teeth chattered. "Bring me another blanket." Mama held me close and gave me quinine, so bitter. She crushed the big white pill on a teaspoon with a little water—then added grape jelly. But I could still taste the bitterness. I gagged and screwed up my face. "I hate mosquitoes!"

Then I fell asleep. My sisters too. We were all in bed for the night. Suddenly I woke and cried, "Mama!" The house was dark and quiet. No one came. "Mama!" I called again. Then I heard distant voices. Laughing, talking.

I crawled out of my crib and ran to the screen door. Across the lawn under the lights coming from the Big House I could see Papa and Mama with their friends playing croquet. There was Uncle Paul and Aunt Ann, Uncle Nathan and Aunt Arlene. That's what we called the other adults even though we weren't related. And since we didn't really know our uncles and aunts back in America, it felt like we had cousins and family around.

Papa and Mama were on a team. They were winning. Papa was such a good shot. "I got you!" I heard him yell to Uncle Paul.

"We're not out of the game yet," Uncle Paul called back. "Ann has a good shot at you."

"Mama," I wailed. "Papa." But they didn't hear. I started to shiver, ran back to my crib and cuddled under the blankets. It was hard to sleep when they were away, but at least I could still hear their voices. They weren't that far away. And the uncles and aunts were there too. Part of the team that ran the hospital and the nursing school.

Every Wednesday night the mission team met for prayer in the Big House where the three nurses lived. We children always went along. The missionaries took turns leading the meeting, reading off a list of prayer requests. We sat in one big circle. Then when it was time to pray, we'd turn around and kneel, propping our elbows on our chairs, heads bowed, our knees cold on the red and black cement floor tiles.

One night I knelt to pray with the group. I slumped down to get comfortable, trying to remember the names of the people we were supposed to pray for. Then suddenly I heard singing. Everyone was sitting up on chairs again except me. Now they'd know I hadn't really been praying. I quickly took my seat, hoping no one noticed. They just kept singing, "When the roll is called up yonder, I'll be there."

At least I'd woken up in time for the roll call! We children ran outside to play. Shivering with fear we held hands and yelled into the darkness, "No bears out tonight. Papa shot them all last night." We snuck off the porch base looking for the elusive "bear-boy" hidden in the shadows. I could run fast. I'd be the last child to escape the scratchy tag of the bear pack. That was the best part of prayer meeting.

3

The First Five Years

Rest time in the tropics is as regular as the sunrise. Mama said I had so much energy that I never felt sleepy and hated those forced naps. Papa usually came in to help us settle and took turns napping beside either Betty or Margaret. I wanted him to take a turn napping with me, but he couldn't because I still slept in a crib.

"Who shall I sleep beside today?" Papa asked.

"I want to sleep by myself!" Betty said.

"So do I," Margaret followed suit. "I'm a big girl now. I don't need anyone to settle me down."

"No one wants me to sleep beside them?" Papa asked.

"I want you, Papa" I said.

"Sorry, Jewel, but your crib's too little. It has to be Betty or Margaret. They've got room in their beds."

Both girls held out, so Papa grabbed a pillow and stretched out on the braided rug in the middle of the cool cement floor.

I cried with shame. How could my sisters be so cruel to Papa? They were soon sniffling too, and both begged Papa to stretch out beside them, but it was too late. Soon we heard Papa's melodious snores rising undisturbed from his floor bed. He could sleep anywhere. And we slept too. I always felt secure when I heard Papa snore. That meant he was home and not off on a trip down country to supervise all the new schools the mission had started.

After naps we ran outside to play with Teddy, our brown mongrel. He rolled over on his back and let me scratch his tummy until he caught a glimpse of one of the stray cats that prowled around. He was off chasing the cat up a big flat-topped Achaia tree outside our front door.

I grabbed an orange from the kitchen. Mama poked a hole in one end so I could suck out the juice. I was only a few yards from the house when suddenly a big black hawk dived down to snatch the orange from my hands. I dropped the orange and ran screaming to the house. The hawk perched on a telephone pole eyeing his prize that rolled to a stop near the sidewalk.

"I didn't know hawks do things like that," Mama said. "He must be really hungry." We watched from the window as the hawk swooped down to claim the orange, and I got a fresh one from the kitchen.

Another day Papa dragged home a big cardboard refrigerator box thinking it would make a nice playhouse for his girls. He was right. We moved in and furnished the place with pillows and blankets—even a potty for indoor plumbing. When dusk drove us in for supper, we didn't want to leave our new home on the front lawn and begged to spend the night.

Papa thought that might be okay, but Mama remembered that sometimes hyenas roamed the grounds. "Please, please, let us try," we begged.

I had a bold idea, "If a hyena sticks his nose in here, we'll just hold the potty up, and he'll run away!" That must have persuaded Mama because we bedded down for the night in the refrigerator box.

Lots of giggles, snacks, trying to decide who should sleep where. Then we heard a noise. I grabbed the potty. We saw something pushing in through the cardboard flap of a door. It had spots like a leopard. We screamed!

Then the leopard laughed and rolled over. It was Uncle Dan, our neighbor and director of the mission. He'd plotted with Papa to don his leopard skin to scare us. The whole compound entered the conspiracy. But that did it. Mama had her way. We moved inside for the rest of the night so the hyenas and leopards could prowl the grounds at will.

I loved to lay in bed at night and listen to the hyenas howl as they scavenged around the town. First, I'd hear the throaty howls that started low and slid up-scale in a tingling twist that chilled my bones. I flung the blanket over my head and listened as the howls came closer and closer. Then the dogs joined the cacophony with menacing barks. Safe inside their thorn-walled compounds the dogs dared the hyena pack to keep its distance. But the hyenas ruled the night, and they knew it.

One night Papa shook me awake. "Jewel, do you want to see a hyena?" I rubbed the sleep from my eyes. I'd only ever heard them. He carried me to the dining room window and there—just four feet away—stood a large hyena eyeing the head of a deer Papa had nailed above the kitchen door. The hyena looked up at the prize that his jaws longed to crush. I was so excited, I leaned in and bumped the window. Spooked, the hyena vanished into the night.

Our house helper, a kindly Ethiopian woman, "Mamete", wondered why we liked that smelly old deer head over the kitchen door. Why would anyone want to attract hyenas? But she was getting used to our strange foreign ways—like how we drank so much milk and used lots of sugar—both expensive delicacies in her world.

Several times a week a farmer came to sell us his milk, but Mama was sure he sometimes added water to the milk he delivered in green glass jars. Sometimes the milk went sour too soon. The milkman didn't have a refrigerator.

"You want milk fresh, sweet?" the farmer asked, surprised. He loved his milk thick, curdled, and smelling of smoke from a calabash hung over a wood fire.

Slowly we began to understand one another's strange ways. One day we went to a wedding feast. Colorful enamel-plated metal containers lined the long table—each filled with a different kind of spicy stew (*wat*). There was chicken *wat,* mutton *wat,* beef *wat,* yellow lentil *wat,* red lentil *wat,* chickpea *wat,* vegetable *wat.*

A gray, spongy crepe-bread (*injera*) lay folded beside my plate. I liked my plate. It was enamel-covered metal with bright blue swirls.

I was hungry and scooped up the spicy chicken leg with the sour crepe. Then I needed a drink. Bad. Immediately. My mouth burned like fire, but no one seemed to notice. Tears came to my eyes. My nose ran. Where were the drinks? We were guests and had to be polite. Quickly I bunched up the front of my full cotton skirt and stuffed it in my mouth. I puffed out my cheeks and rubbed my burning tongue over the cool cotton fabric. That helped smother the fire.

Mama looked at me. "Jewel, don't stuff your skirt in your mouth!" But she knew why. Soon Papa found some orange Fanta. He popped off the lid. It rolled onto the dirt floor into the corner of the tent. The Fanta sure helped, and soon I wanted more *wat*.

It was fun to eat with my hands. We'd take pieces of the *injera* to scoop up the *wat*. The *injera* was smooth on one side but pocked with bubbles on the other. It was like your fork, your spoon and your napkin. When your fingers got messy you just wiped them on another piece of *injera*—and then you ate that too.

I loved to go to the kitchen at the hospital near our home and watch the cook make the stacks of *injera* for all the hospital patients and staff. She'd build a hot fire of kindling under a round concave grill (*mitad*) about 18 inches wide. Then she'd rub the *mitad* with an oily cloth to keep the *injera* from sticking. Next she dipped a bent tin can into a huge barrel of fermented *injera* batter made with gray *teff* flour. Then she poured the batter in concentric circles beginning on the outside edge and coming in until it filled the whole *mitad*. She popped a lid on until steam no longer seeped from the edges, then with one deft twist she slipped a woven straw disc under the finished *injera* and flopped it on top of the stack of *injeras* cooling nearby.

I was mesmerized by the graceful swirls of the cook's arm as she produced the staple food of Ethiopia. Then she gestured to me. "You want to try?" she asked. Sure, I did. It looked so easy, so rhythmic. But it wasn't. I sloshed the batter unevenly—too thick in some places, too thin in others. She took my arm and tried to even things out, then took a spoon to fill in the holes. We laughed and breathed in the smoke of the wood fire while my *injera* baked. Then she folded it up and gave it to me. Soft. Warm. Gray. Sour. I liked American bread, but I liked *injera* too.

I skipped out into the sunlight, heading over toward the pigpen. I arrived just in time to see the workman bringing a huge barrel of slop for the pigs. They smelled it coming and crowded to the side of the pen. Out gushed leftover *injera* and *wat* from hospital trays, potato peelings, orange rinds, onion skins. The pigs squealed and fought to gulp up the garbage. What a life!

Ethiopians don't like pigs and won't eat pork. It's part of their ancient Coptic Christian roots. In fact, the workman almost refused to feed them. But it was a good way to get rid of our garbage from the hospital, and there were Italians and Greeks in town who were glad for the pork.

I decided a pig's life was better than a cow's. Each week, staff at the hospital butchered an ox to provide meat for the hospital kitchen. These were the same oxen we saw pulling single furrow plows through black volcanic soil while farmers yelled and cracked rawhide whips over their patient humped backs.

When their plowing days were done, they got sold at the cattle market—and that's how they ended up with us lowing in protest as they were roped and thrown to the ground on butchering day. One man sat astride the ox's shoulder while another stretched out his head and sliced the throat. The blood gushed out, his bellow a gurgle as life faded from his eyes.

I watched as workmen skinned the carcass, filled corrugated metal tubs with large chunks of meat and bone, then left the innards for the circling vultures. After a thorough scraping with sharp knives, the hide went to the tannery.

It was even more fun watching them kill chickens. Sometimes I helped catch the chickens. The butcher would hold the chicken firmly between his knees. He'd stretch its head back and sever it with one quick slice. As the blood began to spurt, he tossed it onto the grass, but the chicken continued to thrash around, beating its lifeless wings in the dirt. It scared me. One time a dead chicken flopped onto my bare feet spraying them with blood. I ran away. But returned. How could it still move when it was dead?

One day as our dog Teddy napped in the shade of the pick-up truck a man jumped in and began to back up. Teddy howled in pain as the tire ran over his leg. The man realized his mistake and apologized for hurting our dog.

Me with Teddy and Betty with our pet monkey.

As we wailed and watched from the sidelines Papa went to help Teddy, to see if he could fix his leg. But in his pain and confusion Teddy turned on Papa and bit him. Now the doctor said that Papa would need rabies shots. Papa knew Teddy only bit him because he was hurt, but when Teddy died from his injuries the next day, Papa knew he'd need to get the shots—horrible big needles in his stomach for long days in a row. I felt sorry for him but didn't want him to get rabies either.

Mama said there's no cure for rabies. Once you get it you're finished, and you go around biting other people and giving them rabies too until you die. So I was glad Papa got the shots and that they worked.

But I just didn't understand how medicine worked. Every so often Mama would give us Epsom salts to drink. It was supposed to clean us out, get rid of worms and parasites the doctor said we had. One morning Mama poured out a tall glass of Epsom salts with water for me to drink. Betty and Margaret drank theirs straight down and ran out to play, but I couldn't drink mine. Every time I tried it made me gag. Then I had an idea.

"Mama, can I go outside to drink my Epsom salts?" I asked.

She was busy because now we had a little brother too. "Okay," she said, "but you don't play until it's all gone."

I sat on the grass by the nasturtium flowers with their bright orange blossoms and funny round leaves. Not seeing anyone around I dashed my Epsom salts into the flower bed. Then I stood and headed into the house empty glass in hand. But Margaret met me with flashing eyes.

"Mama," she yelled. "I saw Jewel dump her Epson salts into the flower bed." I'd forgotten there was a window.

"Jewel, I can't believe you did that." Mama steered me firmly back to the table as she stirred up another glass of Epsom salts. "Sit there until it's all gone."

I held my nose and downed the repulsive brew in three giant swigs under her watchful eye. Die, worms, die, I thought to myself. It's either you or me.

But there were more things to be worried about than disobedient children. My little brother Chet had been playing with Papa's big ring of keys for the whole hospital compound and lost them. We looked everywhere. Papa raked the yard and the orchard. We searched through all our toys and under all the couches and chairs. Nowhere to be found.

Had someone stolen them? Were we safe at night? Would we need to put new locks on all the dwellings and even the hospital storage rooms? I'd overhear my parents discussing the situation. Every night we prayed God would help us find the missing keys. Papa said he'd change the locks if he had too. He wanted his family to be safe.

One day some of the nursing students from the hospital came to borrow our thermos jug. They were going down country on a vaccination trip and needed to keep the vaccines cold. Before filling the empty thermos with ice, they shook the jug. There was a loud jingle. The missing keys were found! Now we were safe—and the nursing students could make the babies in the countryside safe from smallpox.

***

Papa told us at supper that he'd met the local witch doctor. Sometimes at night we'd hear the drumming and dancing from his home near our compound. I wondered what they did. Was it sort of like Epson salts, rabies shots or vaccinations—just louder?

"We had a nice talk," Papa said. "He told me that he knows the medicines at our hospital work better than his, but it's his way of making a living."

So maybe our hospital was doing some good. The witch doctor was just trying to help people too. He was doing all he knew how to do. He told Papa he wanted to learn more about our medicine. Maybe he'd come to the nursing school we started at the hospital. Papa was the director.

But we couldn't cure everyone. One night our neighbor, the mission doctor Rohrer Eshleman, came running over to tell Papa that his wife, Ellen, was really sick. We never knew what happened, but she went unconscious and stopped breathing. Papa and all the other men on the compound took turns giving her artificial respiration, but finally they realized there was no hope. Dr. Rohrer said there was nothing else he could do.

I'd seen animals die, but this was different. This was a person like Mama. One day Ellen was so sweet and kind, friendly to us even though she didn't have children of her own. Then suddenly there she was—all white and still in a big wooden box.

They put the box in their living room. It was the duplex right next to ours. I crept up to look more closely. She looked like she was sleeping except she wasn't in PJs. She had on a pink dress with a V-neck. It had little sprigs of rose buds dotted all over it. Her long blond hair was pulled back and parted in the center, tucked under a white mesh prayer covering like all our Mennonite women.

We stood quietly in the background while visitors came to see Dr. Rohrer and tell him how sorry they were his wife had died. Mama was still resting because she'd just given birth to her fifth child, a little girl. We'd named my baby sister Sara Grace, but when Ellen died we changed her name to Sara Ellen, in memory of our beautiful neighbor.

They took Ellen's body to Addis Ababa to bury her in a cemetery there. Now Dr. Rohrer was all alone. He lived beside us, but we didn't see him much. He liked to go hunting down by the Awash River when he wasn't working. That was better than going back to an empty house without Ellen.

4

Bingham Academy

Now the inevitable was happening. Our two years in Virginia were done. We were headed back to Ethiopia. I couldn't stop it—even by crying. I hid in my crepe myrtle tree and watched as Papa and Uncle Amos packed the big station wagon. I pushed back thoughts of boarding school. Maybe Jesus would come back and rescue me, or maybe our ship would sink.

Then I remembered the special trunk Mama had packed with toys, games, and books for our month-long voyage. "Don't come back, Jesus, until after I do my new sticker book," I prayed. "Just right before boarding school. Okay?"

A little brother Mark had joined our family here in Virginia. In 1956 we were now a family of six children. All aboard the freighter in the New York City harbor we watched from the deck as a crane loaded the barrels and trunks for our next five years in Ethiopia.

Betty, Margaret and Jewel getting ready to head off to Bingham Academy.

Then Mama saw something that made her heart stop. That carefully packed trunk of children's surprises and activities for the voyage? We watched helplessly as the loading crane mistakenly grabbed our toy trunk and lowered it deep into the hold of the ship with the other freight. It was supposed to be part of our cabin baggage.

"Chester, isn't there anything we can do?" Mama tugged at his sleeve. "I'm afraid it's too late," Papa said. The crane kept whining as it hoisted other huge shipping containers, even cars and trucks deep down into the hold of the ship on top of our little toy trunk.

Freight being unloaded.

"Look, Mama," Betty said brightly as she tore open a good-bye package our friends at the church had thrust into our hands. We weren't supposed to open it until we got on board. It held a copy of *The Adventures of Danny Meadow Mouse* by Thornton Burgess and a pack of colored pens, our only official "entertainments" for the month.

But Papa was a great storyteller, and we invented "Gugerman," a version of tag where Betty was always "it" and the green deck chair was base. And "Blumpso," a continuous version of tag where crossed legs were always the "base." Some days I'd play Mama and order Betty and Margaret to furnish the house.

"Breakfast time," I'd crow, and Betty would transform into a table while I sat on Margaret's back and ate my oatmeal off Betty's back. Then it was time to read a book. I sat on the Betty-couch and read *Danny Meadow Mouse* once again as Margaret beamed like a lamp from the corner.

The month-long voyage passed quickly. At every port Papa took us exploring. Sometimes to beaches for swimming or to seaside restaurants. We couldn't understand Arabic. It was different from Amharic. In Beruit, my sandwich was made of sharp, smelly cheese. I couldn't eat it and just nibbled at the bread. Children at another table devoured a plate of watermelon wedges. I loved watermelon. But we'd already spent our limited foreign money on smelly cheese.

Then before we knew it, we were back at our old home in Nazareth, Ethiopia, and it was time to pack for boarding school. The school sent lists of needed clothing with instructions. Mama had to label everything with indelible ink for the community laundry or sew on name tags. I didn't like all my clothes smelling of indelible ink. The fumes went right up my nose as Mama penned my name on socks, underpants, dresses, and sweaters. She piled my marked clothes in a small brown suitcase, checking off the list. Jacket and sweater. It was colder in Addis Ababa. And rainy.

I still couldn't tell Mama my biggest fear about boarding school. I was too ashamed. But I think she knew and tried to help. At supper she'd whisper, "Jewel, don't drink so much." You see, I still wet my bed at night. Sometimes. What if I wet my bed at boarding school? She wouldn't be there to remind me not to drink too much, or to strip the bed before my big sisters saw what happened.

I was eight. A big girl. Headed into fourth grade with Margaret. Betty was ready for sixth. Little brother Chet would go into first. Mama said we'd have to try to take care of him. But that would be hard. He'd be in the boys' dorm.

Mama had been a schoolteacher before she got married, and she really wanted to keep us at home for school. That's what she'd done our first five years in Ethiopia. But now she had four school-aged children, and two little ones at home. The mission said we had to go to boarding school.

That's just the way it was done. No exceptions. If you wanted to be a good missionary, you had to show how you put God first and didn't make an idol of your family. Boarding schools were God's gift to take care of the missionary children, to give them a good western education right in the country where their parents worked.

I'd read books about the first missionaries to go to places like China. Some of those children got sent all the way back to America or England and couldn't see their parents for years on end. Some of the parents even got killed or the children died far away in America before the parents even knew they were sick. But God said we mustn't love our families more than we loved him. He came first.

Papa loaded our four suitcases in the pale green VW combi van with dark green trim. Bingham Academy was 60 miles away. We climbed out of the Nazareth valley up to the 8,000-foot altitude of the capital city. It was the dry season. Clouds of dust blurred our departure.

I pressed my nose against the dusty van window. It was happening. This big thing. I braced myself against the seat but couldn't hold it back. It felt like a whirlwind sweeping in and picking me up, swirling me away from everything familiar. I couldn't escape. Papa. Mama. Sisters. Brothers. Scattered, blown away like so much dust. Always floating. Never really landing anywhere.

Papa slowed to nose through a huge flock of goats and sheep that flowed around the van. The angry little goatherd yelled and waved his rod as parts of his flock bolted for the nearby gully. I looked back through the dust as he frantically tried to round up his scattered sheep.

We'd messed up his day. He wasn't happy. But neither was I. Soon we'd be at boarding school, and I'd have to leave my parents. Could I bolt like the goats, find a hidden gully back under the thorn bushes?

When we arrived, Papa parked the van and picked up my suitcase. I clung to Mama's hand and buried my face in her full skirt. The big wooden school door swung open and a tall lady with thin black hair greeted us. She smiled at Mama. "Welcome to Bingham Academy. So you're the little Mennonite children? I'm Mrs. Wallace, the head-mistress here."

Her smile didn't last long. It was sharp and scary. When she turned her head I saw two long pins poked into a tight French twist that snaked up the back of her head. Her small brown eyes looked like dark raisins poked into a puffy white sugar cookie.

She gave us a tour of the school spouting information like a spigot. "The bell's just about to ring for supper. That's the dining room...the girls' dormitory is here, the boys' dorm there. Our apartment is up-stairs."

She droned on telling Mama all the rules. "This door is only for guests. Wake-up at 6:30. Morning prayers at 7:00. The children mustn't be late or we'll pour cod liver oil in their oatmeal."

She turned to me, "You'll soon get used to school." I could tell she was trying to sound cheerful, but it didn't work. "Why don't you run off to the dorm with the other girls? What's your name? Jewel? That's different. Do you know how to braid your own hair?" She reached out to touch one of my long brown braids. I shrank from her touch.

"It'll take a long time to braid that hair in the morning. Did you ever consider cutting their hair?" She addressed the question to my mother as though I wasn't there. "It'll take a long time for them to get ready in the morning, and they can't be late for devotions."

Cut our hair? But long hair was part of who we were. Most of the other girls had short bobs. But we were Mennonites. We believed that long hair was a woman's glory. The Bible said so. And we followed the Bible, even if it felt weird. Daniel got thrown in the lion's den for obeying God and praying three times a day. That's harder than braiding long hair.

The supper bell rang. A jarring sound. Tearing us apart. "Come, don't be late," Mrs. Wallace yanked my arm. "You'll sit here with the little girls." She spun on her heels to herd children into the dining room.

My sweaty hand slid from Mama's grasp. I crowded on to the end of a backless bench with Margaret. Betty sat with the big girls at another long wooden table. Chet with the little boys. I could still see Mama and Papa standing in the dining room doorway—watching.

We bowed our heads for grace. I didn't want to close my eyes, to lose sight of them even for a minute. But I had to. Papa said we must always close our eyes in prayer. To see God and shut out the world. When I opened my eyes, they were gone!

"Take some bread," an older girl shoved a platter into my hand. "Welcome to hash and trash." She passed me a dish of stuffed squash. "Buck up. You'll soon get used to it."

I wiped my eyes on my dress sleeve. It smelled like dust. Where was I?

"Now it's time to get changed into PJs before bedtime stories," the older girl, Gloria, coached me. "You'll be my bottom bunker."

That night, lonely and homesick, I cried myself to sleep. The other girls laughed and joked. They seemed to feel at home. Would that ever happen to me? Could I ever make friends, feel at home in this place?

That night I dreamed I was home in my own bed. Mama tucked me in, stopping by my top bunk for a kiss. She smoothed back my long hair. Then I jolted awake. Something warm ran down my legs. I'd wet the bed! Not very much. Maybe it would dry by morning and no one would ever know. I stretched my knees apart and tented the blanket to allow air flow. When the wake-up call came at 6:30 everything was dry. Maybe it was just a bad dream. I made up my bed.

On Saturday morning Mrs. Wallace stalked in. "Everyone strip off your sheets. Put your top sheets on the bottom and throw your bottom sheets on the laundry pile." She handed out clean top sheets.

Then she saw my sheet with a big yellow splotch. It was heaped with all the other sheets. Her beady brown eyes roved the room. "Who wet their bed?" No one spoke up. I couldn't. I wouldn't.

"Was it you," Gloria whispered in my ear. She must have smelled it.

"No," I shrugged. "My sheet was dry."

"We don't know," Gloria answered for me. "All the sheets were dry when we stripped the beds."

"I'll let it go this time," Mrs. Wallace said sternly. "But if you ever wet the bed again, don't cover it up! Come and tell me. Be sure to tell the truth. I'll not have you lying to me!"

Now I knew the rule and was extra vigilant. Every time I used the bathroom I'd reach back and touch the flush tank behind me to reassure myself that I was really in the bathroom and not in my bed. On many occasions in the middle of the night as I dreamed I needed to pee, I'd reach back to touch the flush tank and wake myself up in time to get to the bathroom.

Before long I got into the rhythm of rising at 6:30, morning devotions at 7, breakfast at 7:30 and class at 8:00.

Breakfast was a glass of lumpy powered milk made with warm, chlorinated water and a bowl of oatmeal or cream of wheat seasoned with a teaspoon of brown sugar. As we ate, a teacher came around with a pitcher of cod liver oil. We turned to stick out our spoons as she came by. If we didn't get our spoons out quick enough, she dumped the fish oil into our cereal. Of course, we had to clean up our bowls before we left the table.

Although I was new to all the routines, I soon fell in stride, picking up the mood of the other students. If only the cereal could have been a little warmer—like at home when we had hot cereal, but it was cold and congealed in the bowl. I especially dreaded the mornings we had cold cream of wheat. It made me gag.

Sometimes we had homemade yogurt made in little glass baby food jars and flavored with a teaspoon of sugar. That was good. Then it was off to class.

Right before morning recess one of the kitchen helpers brought us a snack. Sometimes it was my favorite—a handful of warm peanuts and raisins. Sometimes it was a peeled carrot, half a banana or a glass of warm, lumpy powdered milk, my least favorite.

After lunch we had an hour of rest—then back to class for the afternoon.

School was alright, but it was the long hours after school and in the evenings when we missed our families the most. Sometimes we'd play softball or climb on the wooden jungle gym. There were games of fox and geese and prisoners' base.

We liked to explore the eucalyptus woods around the school and build roads, tunnels, and bridges for our dinky toy cars and trucks. Sometimes we tunneled in the brush that lined the riverbank creating houses and forts.

One Saturday two horses showed up grazing on the playground. Without asking permission, which we were quite sure would not be granted, some of us decided to try riding bareback.

There were so many rules at Bingham—which doors to come in and out of, how many pieces of toilet paper and how much toothpaste, no talking after lights out, no talking or sitting up during rest hour, no dessert if you spilled your water...

Whenever we found something there wasn't a rule against—even if we knew it was most likely off limits—we brazenly did it. Here were two perfectly good horses with no rules against riding them.

I loved to read stories of Native Americans like Crazy Horse who rode bareback over the prairies. I unhitched the rope bridle of one of the horses and led him to the steps of the classroom building where my friend Nonnie helped hoist me up on to the horse's bareback. Suddenly he was off at a trot. I clung to his mane and the rope halter, digging my knees into the horse's back, urging him on. I couldn't believe the difference as the jolting trot broke into a smooth, flowing gallop. I'd never had so much fun.

The horse turned and circled back to the classroom steps where I'd mounted.

"Jewel, can you take me with you this time?" Nonnie asked.

"Sure," I offered, already the experienced rider.

Nonnie clamored up behind me. We were off at a swift, jolting trot. She clung to me—and then I felt us both start to slip. I pulled on the horse's mane, but the thin strands slipped through my fingers. We both tumbled off as the horse sped away.

We picked ourselves up and realized we hadn't broken any bones. We rubbed our bruises and walked back to the steps where the horse waited patiently.

"You made me fall off," I said. "From now on you're riding by yourself!"

"I know," she said. "I couldn't help myself. There was nothing else to grab."

Nonnie walked back to the dorm still rubbing her sore arms while I galloped around the field. I'd discovered a new love and started dreaming of having a horse of my own someday.

As I walked back to the dorm I noticed a large haystack that had been moved beside the back door. Maybe that's what the horses were all about. It looked like a building project was underway. Workmen had dug a pit for mixing mud and straw for plaster (*chicka*) over a mesh of woven branches and timbers.

The haystack looked like an inviting slide. I ran into the dorm and called a couple friends. "Come, let's slide down the haystack!"

"I'm sure it's against the rules," said one good little girl.

"I've never heard a rule against sliding down a haystack," I challenged. "There's rules about toilet paper and toothpaste, but not about haystacks. Come on!"

Soon a group of us were climbing up the haystack and sliding down, scattering straw all over the yard. But our fun was short-lived. Mrs. Wallace emerged from the kitchen.

"Girls, girls, stop it. Stop it!" she yelled, her puffy cheeks flushed. "Who told you, you could slide down the haystack? Look, you're scattering straw all over the yard."

I brushed straw from my long brown braids and came up to Mrs. Wallace. "I'm sorry. We didn't know it was wrong," I spoke for the group. "We never heard any rule about not sliding down a haystack."

"Well, it just got moved here yesterday," she sputtered. "You should have known better."

***

Every Sunday afternoon we gathered in the dining hall to write letters to our parents. We lived in Nazareth, a 60-mile, two-and-a-half-hour trip over dusty gravel roads. We were some of the lucky ones, getting to go home about one weekend a month. Children who lived further down-country often saw their parents only during the summers and over Christmas holidays. The handwritten letters kept us in touch.

Some weeks I struggled with what to write home. Once I copied out all the verses of the new Easter song we were learning just to fill up the page, but this Sunday I had a lot to tell. I described my horse riding adventures in vivid detail.

Mrs. Wallace read all the letters before mailing them. This week she pursed her lips as she read mine. She came toward me.

"Jewel, you'll have to rewrite your letter."

"Why?" I asked.

"When your parents read this about you falling off the horse, they'll think we're not taking very good care of you. It'll distract them from the work that God has called them to. They'll worry about you here at Bingham. You have to rewrite the letter, and don't say anything about falling off the horse."

I sighed and started chewing on the end of my pencil. What else was there to write about? Besides, I thought my parents would want to know that I was becoming like Crazy Horse.

The Mennonite Mission team on retreat at Bingham Academy, 1960.

5

An Ever-present Father

Papa and me.

I loved when we got to go home to Nazareth for the weekend. Away from boarding school. Each time I hoped I'd never have to go back. But I always did.

One Sunday afternoon when it came time to return to boarding school, I couldn't stop crying.

We'd had a splendid weekend at home—picnicking at the Hippo Hole, fishing where hot springs emptied into the Awash River, watching monkeys scamper through the big sycamore fig trees lining the river. I'd stood up over the cab of the pick-up chevy truck lined with bench seats while the night wind whipped my braids out like banners. I'd squinted into the wind with watery eyes as the truck rushed home in the dark.

Mission truck used for picnics and hunting trips.

I belonged here in this truck bed. This was my family. These were my people. We rounded a sharp bend and the surging inertia almost flung me off the side. I gripped the steel pipe that held up the truck bed canopy as my sisters crushed against me. We laughed and righted ourselves.

But now, waiting for the VW van that would take us back to school, I was cowed, sobbing. The final goodbyes rip apart what was meant to be together. Maybe if I cried hard enough they'd let me stay home, think I was sick.

"Jewel, why are you crying so hard?" Papa drew me into his lap. We'd already done this parting thing numerous times, but it wasn't getting any easier. It always felt like a fresh wound. Like pulling off a scab before the skin heals. My tears flowed like blood.

"Papa, I'm afraid. I'm afraid that Jesus will come back. And he won't find me in boarding school." Here at home I felt safe. Secure. Where my family went, I went. But 60 miles away? In a strange school where I didn't belong? And besides, I'd lied about my wet bed sheet. The ragged yellow splotch mushroomed before my eyes. Maybe I wasn't good anymore. And I hated Mrs. Wallace.

"Jewel, Jesus always knows where you are. He is with you always. God is your Heavenly Father. I'm sorry I can't be with you all the time, but God is a Father from whom you will never be separated." He stroked my hair, smoothing back the messy strands that had strayed from my two thick braids. He wiped the tears from my eyes. "God loves you more than I ever could!" He gave me a hug and set me down as the VW van filled with other missionary kids honked outside the gate.

I waved goodbye then scooted into the van pressing my nose against the window. I watched through the swirling dust as the long brick duplex faded from sight. I strained to see the last splashes of the brilliant purple bougainvillea vining over our door trellis. Tears gushed from my eyes tracing wiggly lines down the dusty window. I tried to stop crying. It hurt too much.

"Is she always such a crybaby?" Larry punched my little brother Chet in the arm. He shrugged. Maybe boys didn't have feelings like girls. We turned out onto the main street. Home was gone. I couldn't see the oleander bush hedge anymore. The brilliant pink flowers and slender spikey leaves.

Just yesterday I'd lain on my top bunk and watched masked yellow weaver birds poking long strands of grass into their freshly woven basket nests slung to the tips of the tallest oleanders. Birds didn't have to leave home. They'd stay and lay their eggs in the little baskets and the babies would rock to sleep with the breeze.

But I had to leave my home. God with me always? I wanted to believe, but I needed to feel arms. I buried grimy fists in my eyes trying to plug a fresh fountain of tears. Then I made a decision. I'd never cry again. That was the only way to shut off the waterfall. I'd be tough. No one would ever know that I minded leaving home. I'd show them I was strong. I wouldn't have to hurt—ever again. Not at boarding school. Not at home. Never. If I was strong enough to ride a horse all by myself and keep from falling out of a pick-up truck, I was strong enough to stop crying.

So I slid back into the boarding school routines. But something shifted. I'd never cower in the background anymore. I'd take charge.

The next time I lay fretting in the compulsory rest hour, I decided to liven things up. Oh, I wouldn't break any rules. I was too smart and sly for that. I wouldn't sit up or even prop my head up with my elbow. Lying flat on my back I pitched my teddy bear up into the air. I caught him, then sent him somersaulting in the air. Front flips. Back flips. Soon the whole dorm was snickering.

None of us were talking or sitting up. We'd not broken any rules, but the giggles brought Mrs. Wallace to the dorm.

"Were you sitting up?" She queried.

"No," we all answered truthfully.

"Were you out of bed or talking?" Again we had all been obeying the letter of the law. Not knowing what else to do, she delivered a stern warning and left the dorm.

Now teddy bears and other stuffed animals livened rest hour almost every day. Things escalated. We started playing catch with teddy bears and wadded up socks—pitching them from bunk to bunk. We whispered and even got out of bed to retrieve the bears when we fumbled a catch.

It was so much fun we gave up trying to play within the rules and declared all-out war. We knew we'd to be caught, but it was worth it. As the noise and commotion rose Mrs. Wallace strode in scowling.

"You girls know the rest hour rules! I was trying to get some work done in the kitchen. Now I'll have to spank you. God holds me accountable for your behavior. Get out and kneel beside your beds. Everyone of you. It looks like the whole dorm was involved. I'll have to go fetch my strap. I just wish you'd use more self-discipline."

As soon as she left I flipped out of the top bunk to await the coming doom beside the bottom bunk. Then I had a brilliant idea. Sometimes Mrs. Wallace grabbed our dresser-top hairbrushes for handy swats at offenders.

"Everyone get your hairbrush," I ordered. "Let's kneel beside our beds and as soon as she comes in we'll all start smacking our own bottoms."

We giggled and grabbed our brushes. As soon as Mrs. Wallace entered the room, the three-inch wide leather strap dangling over her arm I looked up and said as sweetly and submissively as I could,

"We're trying to obey you, Mrs. Wallace, and use self-discipline." And we all applied our brushes to our own bottoms.

A broad smile spread across her puffy cheeks. A rare sight. "Girls, girls, you are just too funny. I guess I won't spank you this time. Get back into bed and no more talking until rest time is over."

Soon after this we were caught giggling after lights out at bedtime. When Mr. Wallace turned off the school generator at 9 pm each evening, eerie calm and cloying darkness settled like chilly dew. Giggling helped you know that you weren't alone in the dark.

But Mrs. Wallace heard the giggles. We knew she was on the way to investigate as we saw the circle of light arcing from the hissing pressure lantern that swung from her fist.

"Girls, I'll be back to deal with this in a few minutes. You really must settle for the night."

The hissing light receded and undercover of darkness my top bunker Jeanie quickly grabbed three extra pairs of underpants from her dresser drawer to pull on as padding.

But all too soon Mrs. Wallace returned, and our bunk was first in line.

"Get out and kneel beside your beds," Mrs. Wallace ordered.

I heard rustling overhead and wondered what was taking Jeanie so long. This was asking for trouble. "Just a minute, please," Jeanie begged.

But Mrs. Wallace wasn't having it. She flung back the covers and dragged Jeanie to the floor.

That's when I saw what had happened. In her hurry to don the extra underpants she'd crammed two legs down one hole on the last pair and ran out of time to pull on her PJ bottoms to cover her ruse.

I couldn't help nearly giggling through my strapping as I got off easy coming on the heels of Jeanie's encounter and the extra wrath and energy expended on her.

Jewel leads orchestra at a Bingham Academy music program.

6

Fitting In

By now I'd become more adjusted to boarding school. Good friends, like Jeanie, and the fun of outsmarting Mrs. Wallace helped me feel powerful and more in control. It was gratifying to feel like we'd get the upper hand once in a while. Yet too often I felt suffocated—like I was in a dust storm and couldn't breathe.

And it wasn't only me. One day my friend Barbara saw there was mashed papaya with lime juice for dessert. Now when papaya is mashed, it gets slimy. Barbara said it made her gag. She hated papaya day. We all knew the punishment for spilling your water at the table. No dessert. Well, thought Barbara, since I don't like papaya, I'll just "accidentally-on-purpose" spill my water.

But hawk-eyed Mrs. Wallace happened to know that Barbara hated papaya. And she just happened to see her push over her water glass. She marched Barbara over to a small table in the corner and shoved two bowls of mashed papaya under her nose.

"You'll sit right there until you eat both bowls of papaya—even if it takes you all day and all night," she said.

Lunch over, we filed quietly out to the dorms for rest hour. But I wanted to stay with Barbara, to help her eat that slimy papaya. I didn't mind it that much. Mrs. Wallace was so cruel. Poor Barbara held her nose and gagged after each bite. Tears gushed from her eyes. I remembered when Mama made me drink my Epsom salts after I dumped the first batch in the nasturtiums, but she didn't make me drink two glasses full. It just wasn't fair.

Another day before rest hour, I went to the door and peaked out at a mother dog. She'd just delivered a litter of puppies beside the dorm's porch steps. The brown and white mother curled contentedly in a cardboard box nursing her litter. I climbed onto my bunk and lay there wondering what it would feel like to have children someday. I grabbed my pillow and nestled it against my chest.

That was when Mrs. Wallace burst into the dorm. She came straight to my top bunk, her square heels hitting the floorboards like mallets.

"Sit up," she ordered. "Don't you know it's wrong to go outside in your slip?" She slapped her broad hand down with a stinging smack on my bare thigh as I sat dangling my legs over the edge of the bunk.

"But I didn't go outside in my slip," I said with a puzzled frown. During rest hour we always took off our outer dresses and napped in our slips so as not to wrinkle our dresses.

"Don't lie to me! I saw you with my own eyes," she yelled, raining blows on my now-crimson thighs. "I'll keep this up 'til you tell the truth!"

I didn't want to lie. I knew that wasn't right. Ever since I'd lied about wetting the bed I determined to always tell the truth. But what she was doing wasn't right either. My mind scrambled to find an honest way out of the dilemma, but as the slapping continued, I finally managed a feeble, "Okay," and the slapping stopped.

"What was that all about?" I whispered to my friend in the neighboring bunk as Mrs. Wallace retreated to the kitchen.

"Remember when you peeked out the door at the puppies? Mrs. Wallace must have been in the pantry and seen you," she said.

So that was going outside in my slip? I slitted my eyes, refusing to cry. Hate for Mrs. Wallace welled up like a volcano. Someday. Someday. When I grew up. When I was in control. I'd show her what it feels like to get hit.

For now, she was in charge. I'd bide my time. But there'd be ways to get revenge.

One afternoon during the rainy season we discovered dozens of tiny tree frogs swarming the woods outside our dorm. We filled a large tin can with handfuls of frogs. Then knotted a bandana over the top to keep them from bouncing out.

"Let's let frogs loose during study hall," I suggested to Nonnie. This was another one of those totally boring hours—like rest hour. Only this time we sat quietly in the dining hall doing homework. Nonnie agreed to my plan, so we brought the can of frogs into the dorm and placed it on a high shelf in the closet.

After supper and before study hall we brushed our teeth, donned PJs, and bathrobes. That way we were ready to slide quickly into bed after study hall when Mr. Wallace cut off the generator. Both Nonnie and I placed a couple little frogs in our bathrobe pockets.

That evening we studied more diligently than ever—not wanting Mr. Wallace, the study hall supervisor, to suspect anything. Fifteen minutes in, I locked eyes with Nonnie at the table across the room. I gave a little nod signaling that this would be great time to release the first frog.

She shook her head ever so slightly and turned back to her writing. Another 15 minutes slipped by. Then another. Neither of us wanted to take the risk. Finally, during the last quarter, I decided it was now or never. I plunged my right hand into the soft chenille bathrobe pocket and gathered one little frog into the crook of my three small fingers. I slowly drew out my hand and pinched a pencil between my thumb and first finger, pretending to write. Then I flipped my pencil off the table. As I reached down to retrieve the rolling pencil, I opened my fingers to set the little frog free.

Glad to be released from his prison, the tiny frog began hopping toward the door of the study hall. Nonnie smiled. Other students caught on and grinned.

Then we all heard an unusual sound for that time of night. A car pulled up to the front of the school, tires scrunching in gravel. Mr. Wallace heard it too and went to the door. Soon we heard his greeting. "Oh hi, Mr. Hay. What a surprise and pleasure to see you at this hour."

My heart sank. Mr. Hay was the director of the Sudan Interior Mission that ran Bingham Academy. He had chosen this very evening to come for a visit. We didn't have phones, so of course he couldn't call ahead.

Soon both men strode toward the study hall. Mr. Hay would want to greet us kids. He worked with many of our parents and decided who did what. He'd send some missionaries way down country where they wouldn't see their kids for nine months at a time. Then others, like Mr. and Mrs. Wallace, got to stay with their kids since they worked at Bingham.

My little frog was hopping right toward Mr. Hay and Mr. Wallace. I'd have given anything to put the frog back in my pocket, but it was too late.

The men kept coming and then—crunch. Mr. Hay stepped right on top of my little frog. He was a big man, and that step smashed the little frog into unrecognizable smithereens.

"Humm," he paused. "What was that? Must have been a little bit of food." He scraped the bottom of his shoe on the wooden floorboards and kept walking. The bell rang. Study hall over, we hurried to our dorms.

Usually, Mrs. Wallace said good night and rushed away with the hissing pressure lantern as soon as she saw us kneeling down for bed-time prayers. Tonight, she'd probably have to meet with Mr. Hay after we were all in bed. But for some strange reason she lingered, watching us. Her eyes, glistening in the lantern light, roved the darkened dorm. Just as I got up from my knees and began to slip into bed, Nonnie bent over and whispered, "Don't scream when you get in bed."

Gingerly I slid between the sheets and slowly explored the bottom surface of the bed with my feet and hands. Something cold and wet wiggled. I froze, shut my eyes, and lay like the dead until finally Mrs. Wallace said, "Good night, girls," and left with the lantern.

Then I gathered the little frog into the palm of my hand and crept to the window. "Good night, little soldier," I whispered into the dark.

"I'll let you escape with your life. You can be free—even if I'm not. You belong in the woods. That's your home. Go find your mama. Or maybe it was mama that got stepped on in the study hall—a martyr for the cause!" I threw him out the window.

7

Things Get Worse

One weekend I went home. We'd had another picnic down by the river. By now I was in seventh grade, one of the big girls at boarding school. It still hurt to leave home, but not as much as it used to. Not since I'd learned how to stuff my feelings and shut off the tears.

I walked into the dorm that Sunday afternoon feeling like a conqueror. Just one more year and then I could leave Bingham forever. Papa told us we were going to start our own school along with some other mission groups. Bingham didn't have room for the Mennonite children anymore, and that was fine with me.

I loved my friends at Bingham—Nonnie, Jeanie, and Marilyn. I couldn't wait to tell them about the fish we'd caught, the huge crocodile we'd spotted sunning on the bank near the fishing hole. Crocs knew where to find the fish too.

"Hi, I'm back," I yelled as I swung the brown suitcase onto my bunk.

No one greeted me. Stifled sobs rose from the surrounding bunks. Nonnie's eyes were puffy.

"Woah. What went on around here this weekend?" I asked, trying to cheer everyone up.

"We had a water fight," Jeanie said.

"Sounds like fun," I said, knowing I'd have been in the thick of it if I hadn't gone home for the weekend. "What's the punishment this time?"

My friends looked whipped, shamed, and they hadn't even been punished yet. Something was seriously wrong.

"What's she gonna do to you?" I asked.

"She's going to punish us in front of our 'little sisters,'" Marilyn said.

We each had a "little sister" in the little kids' dorm. We helped them dress each morning. My little sister was actually my real sister, Sara.

"How's she going to punish you?" I asked.

"Bare-bottom spankings," she said. "Right in front of them."

All my pent-up rage boiled over. My sense of justice and fair play shot up like a geyser. This was not right. She had stepped over a line. She was going too far.

She'd slapped me crimson for peaking at some puppies forcing me to lie. She'd made Barbara eat two bowls of slimy papaya. She'd strapped me for talking after lights out, made me rewrite my interesting letters home countless times, but bare-bottom spankings in front of our little sisters?

"We can't let her do that," I cried. "This is going too far." I remembered how helpless and lost I'd felt when I first came to Bingham, how cowed and humiliated. But then I'd learned. Learned that I could have friends and fun around the edges of the rules. There had to be a way to get out of this meanspirited punishment.

Suddenly I felt strong. "Wait." I cried. Figuring in my head. "There's more of us. Ten against one. When she comes in here let's jump her, drag her down to the boys' dorm, and give her a bare-bottom spanking!"

Now I wouldn't really have done this. At least I don't think so. I just wanted to cheer them up—to talk big and give a shot of encouragement. I expected to hear the dorm erupt in brave laughter at my brash idea, but it was deathly still. Then I heard a floorboard creak.

I spun around and there stood Mrs. Wallace, her eyes blazing.

She grabbed my chin in her hand, forcing me to look in her eyes. "Just who, Miss Jewel, were you going to drag to the boys' dorm for a spanking?"

"Why, y-you, I suppose," I stuttered, dropping my eyes to the floor where the dark knots in the wooden boards stared back like hollow-eyed children.

"You suppose? Are you going to add lies to slander? I heard you with my own ears." Her sweaty fingers slid off my chin.

"Now go to your bed and wait there 'til I come for you. The rest of you girls who were involved in the water fight, come with me to the little girls' dorm." Her square heels hit the floor like armies marching to the front.

I curled up in bed like a soldier in a bunker. The enemy was advancing. I had no weapons left. From the next room I heard the smack of leather on bare flesh—exploding like bombs. One round then another.

One by one, my friends slunk back to their beds. The first attack was over. We'd not been able to repulse it. We waited in the lull, nursing our wounds. What was next? It had to be something worse. She'd gone over the top. What was left in her arsenal?

The dorm grew still, and then Mrs. Wallace came for me.

"Come here," she ordered. I slid off the bunk and stood before her looking down at her clumpy black shoes with square heels.

"Look at me!" she ordered. "You wanted a chance to strap me? Here it is. Hit me!" She thrust the leather strap into my hands and held out her pasty-white arms—palms up. Flesh sagged like curtains from her upper arms.

Everything in me hated her. She'd strapped me more times than I could remember. She'd just humiliated all my friends. Her huge bosom rose and fell like two giant hills under her forest-green sweater. Not a single strand of black hair strayed from the tight twist stabbed with pins atop her head. She towered over me, a grim smile on her thin lips.

I wanted to kill her, to poke out her eyes with those sharp hair pins. To push her down and stomp on those big green hills. To run away forever—down to the Awash River.

But I knew I couldn't. She was in control. She could do anything she wanted. She was telling me to strap her. What if I really did—with all my might?

Lamely I let the strap fall across her arms. "Harder," she taunted. "Now's your chance."

I ventured another half-hearted blow, then threw the strap down.

"I'm sorry, Mrs. Wallace," I mumbled. "I shouldn't have said that."

"Go to bed," she said abruptly, turned and walked out of the room. I thought I saw a tear in her eye. And I was crying, the first time since I'd turned off my tears in the dust on the way back to boarding school.

8

Good Shepherd School

The group of Mennonite missionary children who attended the newly constructed
Good Shepherd School. Jewel, back left.

Papa and Mama arrived with the VW van to pack up our things. I couldn't believe we were leaving Bingham forever. I looked back as we sped out the lane. I hoped I'd never see Mrs. Wallace again.

That new school, Good Shepherd, was really in the works. Bingham Academy was overflowing and gave preference to children with the Sudan Interior Mission. The other missions were forming their own school, and I couldn't be happier.

Papa and Mama had eight children by now, so schooling was a big deal for us. Papa had pulled together leaders from the Baptists, Lutherans, and Presbyterians to form this new school. Now we could have a voice in some of the school policies and procedures. We could help supply staff members.

But Papa still had to convince Orie O. Miller and the other leaders of the Mennonite Mission. We heard that they'd already decided to fly the Ethiopian missionary children to Tanzania where the Mennonites had built a big school for missionary children.

We met for the mission conference at the Bishoftu Conference Center alongside a round green crater lake, one of seven in the region. At first when we went swimming there we used inner tubes because the lake was deep all the way to the edge—without a beach. But by now I could swim. I hoped I could swim across the lake someday.

While the adults were in their meeting with Orie, we children were free to roam the grounds. Maybe this was my chance to swim across the lake. I tiptoed in to ask Mama's permission.

She looked at me solemnly. "Jewel, God has given you only one life. What you do with it is up to you."

That made me think. If I drowned trying to swim across the lake I'd be gone. Forever. And ever. Maybe it wasn't the wisest thing to do. I'd wait until Papa could come along in a boat. I ran down to see some of the younger children playing in a small cement pool. And I'm glad I did. Little Jean had gotten in over her head and was struggling to get to the edge. I grabbed her hand and pulled her out. Later her mama, Aunt Blanche, thanked me. So I knew I'd made the right decision.

Then Papa told us what had happened in the meeting with Orie. He'd crunched the numbers about how much it would cost to fly all of us kids to Tanzania and back a couple times a year as well as look after us there. Then he figured how much it would cost to build our own school in Ethiopia and keep us kids closer to our parents. Orie probably felt like all the missionary parents ganged up on him. He'd already decided our fate, written the minutes of the meeting before it happened. But Papa's research convinced him to change his mind and that's how Good Shepherd School got started.

Good Shepherd opened the next year even though the dorm wasn't built yet. We stayed in a hostel with the new Baptist principal Gil Anderson and his wife Grace. Every day we drove for half an hour across town to the new classroom building in the country. Now Margaret and I were in eighth grade. We were the big girls.

This was Gil and Grace's first year in Ethiopia, so they were trying to get adjusted as well as start a new school. Gil was the principal and taught math and science. Grace taught music, piano, and choir.

Grace came to Margaret and me. "What do you children want in your lunches?" she asked.

She was asking our advice? That felt good. She wanted to learn from us.

"Oh, peanut butter and jelly is good. Or tomatoes and mayo for the sandwiches," we suggested.

"Is that enough?" Grace wondered. "You don't need meat?"

I liked Grace and the smaller bedrooms in the hostel. It felt more like a home instead of a boarding school. Grace was friendly and laughed when she talked. She wanted to hear what I thought instead of just telling me what to do.

I ventured a question. "Is it okay if we change our dresses before the end of the week?"

She frowned, trying to understand. "You mean, wear a fresh dress and hang the used one back in the closet if it's not dirty?"

"Yes," I said. "At Bingham we had to wear the same dress all week."

"Oh," she laughed, understanding my question. "Sure. You can wear whatever you want. You're a big girl. It's your decision."

I had choices. I could choose my sandwich spread. I could choose my dress.

I skipped outside and ran to the big eucalyptus tree in the corner of the backyard. I wanted to shinny up the smooth mottled trunk with its scaly bark. It was freeing to know that Grace, Mrs. Anderson, wouldn't yell at me or make rules about trees.

I wished I could borrow a pair of my brother Chet's jeans like I had at home one time. I loved to shinny up a smooth straight tree, clamping the soles of my feet to the trunk with legs bent in a frog-like crook. But Mama said wearing jeans made me act like a boy. After donning Chet's jeans one afternoon I'd made the mistake of swaggering around with arms akimbo. So I had to strip off the jeans.

I shouldn't push my new freedoms with Mrs. Anderson too far, so I found three big safety pins and pinned a seam that pulled together the front and back of my full skirt to create billowy pantaloons. That worked and soon I was up the tree peering over the privacy fence into the eucalyptus forest that surrounded our hostel.

A group of kids clustered around the tree. "How'd you get all the way up there?" Benny asked.

I slid down trying not to snag the safety-pinned skirt on the bark. "Just like this." I demonstrated my frog-leg grip that hopped me up the trunk. Then everyone wanted to try. But no one could go as high as I did, not even Benny, the biggest boy.

Margaret and I were the only eighth graders, so we often worked on our own. Mr. Anderson from the Baptist Mission and Mr. Gilbertson from the Lutheran Mission taught the classes. We weren't sure about Mr. Gilbertson. Sometimes he came to school smelling like cigarette smoke. I couldn't believe my nose. Everyone knew Christians didn't smoke. How could he even be a missionary and smoke? Then we heard that Lutherans drank wine, too. I asked my Lutheran friend Elaine if it was true that her father smoked cigarettes and drank wine. She shrugged. "Well, Jesus drank wine."

She wouldn't answer me straight out, so I knew it must be true. There sure were lots of different kinds of Christians, but I was pretty sure Mennonites were the best. We followed the Bible—even the hard stuff.

One time when we were having holy communion with some other missionaries all the adults took bites of bread and sips of grape juice together, but the non-Mennonite missionaries got up and left while the Mennonite missionaries stayed to wash each other's feet.

I asked Mama why the other missionaries didn't stay for the foot washing. Didn't Jesus wash his disciples' feet and tell them this was something they should always do? It showed how they were willing to serve each other even in dirty, smelly ways.

She said, yes, and showed me in the Bible, John 13, where Jesus taught about foot washing. I felt good and warm inside. I wanted to follow Jesus, even if it meant doing hard things. And I wanted to belong to a group of people who washed each other's feet. I'd never get up and leave a foot washing service like those non-Mennonite missionaries. If the Bible said we should wash feet, I'd wash feet.

After the foot-washing we all stood up and sang, *"The Love of God is greater far than tongue or pen could ever tell..."* No one played the piano, but the women sang in soprano and alto, the men in tenor and bass.

The non-Mennonite missionaries who had left without washing feet came back and stood at the door listening to the music. They smiled and clapped for us. I heard Mr. Hay tell Papa he'd never heard such beautiful singing.

It just all went together—our long braids and white mesh prayer veilings, the foot washing, and the four-part acapella harmony.

Back at Bingham sometimes, the other kids had teased us about our prayer coverings and pulled our braids, but I hadn't minded too much. I'd started wearing a covering when Margaret and I got baptized. I remember how Aunt Ann, one of the other missionary women, came up and gave me a big kiss on the cheek and a warm hug. It made me feel like I belonged, like I was part of the family.

When some of the guys saw our coverings they started a little chant—"tackin' on a tarboosh, tackin' on a tarboosh." They said our little white hats looked like "tarbooshes," the white skull caps worn by Muslim men who make the pilgrimage to Mecca. That was news to me. It wasn't a tarboosh. It was a covering, a Mennonite covering! And maybe everyone else should obey the Bible and wear coverings too.

"Oh, you think you're better than everybody else?" John teased as I sat on the merry-go-round. "Your theme song is *'take time to be holy....'*"

But I wasn't feeling very holy and chased him into the underbrush. Back in the dorm I turned a somersault on my top bunk, mashing my covering. Just then Betty walked in and spied my smashed covering askew over my ear. She pinned it back on straight and said, "Jewel, if you want to turn somersaults remember to take your covering off first."

***

Meanwhile back at the hostel we gathered at the breakfast table and Mr. Anderson surprised us with an announcement. "We won't be going to school today. There's been a military coup."

"What's a coup?" I asked.

"When Emperor Haile Selassie left the country on a state visit, his bodyguards seized power. They want to rule the country. But now we hear that army forces loyal to His Majesty are fighting back," Mr. Anderson said. "It's like a civil war, different parts of the country fighting to be in charge."

Soon we began to hear rifle shots and the rattle of machine guns in the distance. The electricity went off. The telephone line went dead. We chatted, not sure what to do with our unexpected freedom. Gil and Grace listened to the short-wave radio.

What if the battle lines came closer? Grace told us all to pack little overnight bags and put them on the ends of our beds. "If the fighting comes closer we can slip out of the city to Ambo. We know Baptist missionaries there who can take us in," she said.

Some of the little girls started crying. "When can we go home?" Marian sobbed. Her parents lived way down country, but I wondered if the trains were even running anymore.

After lunch I organized some group games. We sat around on the living room floor playing "Hot Potato" when suddenly a jet screeched overhead. Boom. A bomb! Then another. Nowhere was safe now. Another bomber. And another.

We huddled on the floor. I grabbed my little sister. Margaret grabbed another little girl. We waited. More bombs. Then Benny sat up ever so slightly and gave me a crooked grin. "Just think of all the stories you'll have to tell your grandchildren," he said.

"Yeah!" I said. "We're having quite the adventure." We wanted to cheer up the little children, to act like we weren't afraid. But inside I was shaking. Would I even live to have any grandchildren? Would the next bomb fall on us? Would I ever see Mama and Papa again?

Darkness came early because there was no electricity. The bombers stopped but the machine guns rattled on. Mr. Anderson read us a bedtime story with a flashlight then we all went to bed huddling together on the floor in case any bullets came in through the windows.

Still no news. Mr. Anderson kept checking the phone line. Dead. The second day dragged on. Then in the afternoon suddenly we heard rifle shots right outside our hostel in the vast eucalyptus woods I'd seen from the tree in our yard.

"Down on the floor everyone," Mr. Anderson ordered, but he wouldn't have had too. We flattened ourselves on the floor wishing it would open up and swallow us, hide us from the soldiers with guns right outside the gate.

We slept on the floor another night. Still no news. At breakfast the next day we ate the remaining bread and jam. Suddenly the phone rang. Mr. Anderson snatched the receiver. As we crowded around, he smiled and nodded, "Will do. Thanks for your call. See you in a half hour."

"The war is over," he said. "That was Dan Sensenig, the director of the Mennonite Mission. He's coming in the mission van and will take all of you Mennonite children to Nazareth. We're dismissing early for the Christmas holidays. His Majesty is back on the throne."

We cheered and ran to pack our bags. When Uncle Dan got there the van had a huge white cross made from adhesive tape spanning the windshield. That meant we were loyal to the emperor and the soldiers with guns who lined the streets waved us past until we got to the open road leading to Nazareth.

9

Never Say Never

Without any missionary boarding schools for high schoolers, when I finished eighth grade at Good Shepherd, Papa and Mama decided that Margaret and I could attend the Bible Academy, an Ethiopian high school the Mennonite Mission had started. That meant I could live at home and walk down the hill to school. It suited me just fine.

That summer I helped Papa plant trees and bushes around the campus. Sometimes we hiked to surrounding hills and picnicked at the Awash River. And I had time to think.

At boarding school I'd taken most of my strappings in stride. It was just the price of living a normal life. But I'd never told Mama and Papa about how Mrs. Wallace made me spank her. That encounter bothered me. I knew I shouldn't have said those mean things—even if she was cruel and unfair. Jesus says we should love even our enemies. That was another thing Mennonites believed. And she sure was my enemy. I just hoped I'd never have to see her again. I could bury her like I did my tears. Never think about her again.

One day as Mama stopped by my bunk at nap time, I told her I needed to tell her something. She was in a hurry so my words just tumbled out. "Mama, Mrs. Wallace gave everyone in the dorm a bare-bottom spanking. When I said we should give her one, she made me strap her."

"Really?" Mama said. "That's strange." Then she bent and kissed me. She stroked my hair. I think she already knew. "You're Second-to-None," she whispered. Relief swept over me like the fragrance of the first rain that breaks the dry season. It was okay. Mama said so. I was home.

A few days later a strange car pulled into our compound. I watched in horrified fascination as a group of SIM missionaries piled out. There was Mrs. Wallace and Mr. Wallace and their three little children along with others I didn't know.

Papa greeted them warmly. "What brings you here?"

Mr. Wallace explained for the group. "We were traveling through, on our way to visit some stations down country. But we heard there's a nice spot to view hippos in the Awash River and thought we'd stop there on the way. Could someone show us the way to the Hippo Hole?"

"We'll see who we can free up," Papa said, stepping back to confer with Mama.

I ran and hid behind the house in the oleander bushes. I didn't want to see Mrs. Wallace ever again. Then I heard Mama call. I came to the back porch.

"Jewel, you know the way to the Hippo Hole. Would you mind going along with the Wallace party to show them the way?" I wished I'd run further—been out of earshot. I'd rather hoe the garden, mop the dusty cement floors.

"Mama, I don't want to," I said.

"Jewel, we think you're the best one to do it," she said. "Margaret can go along too. You can help them have a fun time."

I'd go to please Mama and Papa, not the Wallaces.

"Okay" I agreed reluctantly, flinging back my long braids. Soon Margaret and I found ourselves stuffed in the van with a group of mostly strange adults heading toward the Awash. Now I was in charge. "Turn here. Turn there," I said. And Mr. Wallace turned.

We went to the normal spot, but the hippos had migrated further upriver. The Wallace party never would have found the hippos on their own. I suggested we strike out through the bush following the river since they weren't in their usual spot. Suddenly around a bend in the river, we saw a whole pod of hippos.

The adults were excited, pulling out their cameras and telephoto lenses, shooting pictures. We drove right up to the bank of the river. I'd never seen a better hippo show. The large beasts yawned and snorted. Baby hippos frolicked and dove off their mothers' backs. And the cameras rolled.

"We need to go before it gets dark," I warned Mr. Wallace. He brushed me off.

"Sometimes after dark they close the gate at the entrance," I said again. "We really need to go."

"We haven't eaten our picnic yet," Mrs. Wallace said, passing around sandwiches as the photographers snapped away.

Dusk fell quickly as we packed up and picked our way along the cow paths through gullies and thorn bushes back to the road that led up the side of the mountain. I sank back into my seat, eager to get home and free of my unwanted responsibilities. I was glad they'd had a good time, but I couldn't quite help feeling that they didn't deserve it.

The heavily loaded van turned on to the steep gravel road that angled up the mountain flanking the river gorge. Two-thirds of the way up the mountain, at the steepest part of the slope, two men shouted angrily in Amharic, "Stop. Stop!"

Then I saw it. A metal gate completely blocked the narrow road from the cliff to the mountainside. The van pulled up to the gate and stopped. There was no way around. Mr. Wallace got out, but he couldn't speak Amharic. The two men guarding the gate yelled and motioned to him holding up their fingers. "Twenty dollars. Twenty dollars," they kept repeating. He could understand that much Amharic.

"What?" Mr. Wallace exploded. "I thought you said it was free. We can't pay that much. We're missionaries. That's exorbitant. I won't pay it!"

He got back in the car and revved the motor. Was he going to ram the gate? Force his way through? I cringed and shrank back in my seat wondering what Papa would do. He knew Amharic. He'd talk to the men, try to come to a fair agreement. We had stayed longer than we should have. Now the guards had us trapped and they knew it.

Mr. Wallace tried to start the overloaded van, but the clutch slipped and it drifted closer to the edge of the cliff. He braked in the loose gravel sliding closer to the edge. Mrs. Wallace screamed.

"Let me out, please," I said. "We can all walk up the hill. The van's too loaded to start in the middle of the hill."

"Nonsense," he said. "This van has a good strong motor." And he tried again.

The two guards yelled and banged on the side of the van. "$20. $20 or you'll be here all night."

"Roy, let us walk up the hill." It was the sweetest thing Mrs. Wallace had ever said.

"Okay, Francis. Everyone out."

I burst out into the night air, ducked under the gate, and ran up the hill. The rest of the group followed while Mr. Wallace bickered with the guards. I quickly put as much space as possible between me, the drifting van, and the escalating quarrel. I'd run all the way home if I had to. I'd never get back in that van.

I listened to the murmur of the group as they made their way uphill behind me. Then I heard the rusty metal gate swing on its hinges as it opened downhill. Van tires scrabbled in the loose gravel, then slowly gained momentum until it reached the walkers. All the group boarded, but I kept on running.

Mr. Wallace slowed the van beside me. "Jewel, you need to get in. I paid the guards so we're free to go." He slid the door open and I pressed in beside Margaret.

No one talked. The van lights stabbed the thick darkness of a countryside devoid of electric lights. A half hour later we began to see the lights of the village of Nazareth spread out in the valley. We were almost home.

"It's really gotten late." Mrs. Wallace broke the silence. "But your parents won't worry because they know you're with us."

***

I never saw Mrs. Wallace again. Sometimes I wondered why I hated her so much. I mean, she's a person too. A missionary even. She had kids, a cute little girl named Janice. She had rosy cheeks and was really good at singing. Once Mrs. Wallace even invited us to her apartment above the dorm and served us apples. Apples. We never had apples. They don't grow in Ethiopia, and you have to import them. But she gave us slices of apples.

One evening she'd invited the older girls over for a talk about growing up. They came back and told us all the secrets "Granny Genitals" had revealed.

I listened wide-eyed as Jeanie whispered, "She said that Mr. Wallace puts the thing…," she pointed to her crotch, "into her thing…" She squeezed her thighs together.

"What?" I asked, incredulous. "That can't be."

"But it's true. And Nonnie said her parents do it too." What? This was bizarre, unthinkable! I shook my head.

"I never heard anything so yucky," I said. "Maybe all the SIM missionaries do it, but I'm sure my parents would never do anything like that!" Maybe this was one more way Mennonites were differ-ent—you know, the foot washing, the coverings and long braids, the acapella music, loving our enemies. We read the Bible and tried to follow Jesus every day. Our ancestors even died for their faith. What did the Bible say about stuff like this? That's what I'd like to know.

Well, Mama got wind that we were talking about this at boarding school, so she called us older girls into the bedroom. I tugged at her sleeve. "Jeanie says her parents..." I couldn't bear to finish the sentence. It was too dirty, too yucky. "But I told her you and Papa wouldn't..." I could see from her eyes that in this regard Mennonites were like everybody else, and I hung my head in shame.

10

Goodbye Ethiopia. Hello America

Haile Selassie, hosted by Papa, tours the Bible Academy and quizzes students in their knowledge of the Bible.

T he year at the Bible Academy slipped away. The most exciting thing was the day His Imperial Majesty, Emperor Haile Selassie, stopped by our compound with his entourage. He was pleased that

Papa could speak Amharic and show him around the school without an interpreter.

I held my breath as the king entered the classroom where I sat with my Ethiopian classmates. He turned to Papa, "So you say this is a Bible school where you teach the Bible along with other subjects? Is it okay if I quiz the students in their Bible knowledge?"

"Go right ahead," Papa replied.

"Tell me," the little emperor asked. He stood dwarfed beside my six-foot, two-inch Papa. "What is found in Isaiah chapter 7?"

Now I thought I knew all the Bible stories, but to just pick out a scripture reference and ask what's in it? No way I could answer that question. But one of my classmates raised his hand.

The emperor acknowledged him, and Samuel said, "In chapter 7 the prophet Isaiah tells us that 'a virgin shall conceive and bring forth a son...'" Pleased, and yet still trying to stump us His Majesty tried again.

"Very good. Now, what about Daniel chapter 2?"

My mind went blank, but again Samuel raised his hand. "Are you the only one who knows the Bible?" His Majesty asked with a grin as he scanned the room. Slowly another arm raised.

"In Daniel chapter 2, King Nebuchadnezzar sees a tall image with a head of gold..."

We'd passed the king's test. My heart burst with pride to be part of such a class. How amazing that the king knew his Bible better than I did, and that he wanted the people in his country to read and know their Bibles. Wanting to unify the country, he only allowed the Bible to be translated into the national language of Amharic. But if you wanted to read the Bible in the national language, that was fine.

After just one year at the Bible Academy it was time to go back to America. It had been six years since we'd been there—on our peach farm in Virginia—five years of boarding school and now this year.

Mama fretted about how we girls should dress. If we went to Lancaster Mennonite School we'd have to wear cape dresses instead of skirts and blouses. We'd have to wear nylons and dress shoes. We'd have to put our hair up. No more loose flying braids. I couldn't imagine putting my hair up in a bun, but that could wait. Mama ordered black bonnets for us to wear for the trip home. "That's what Mennonites wear when they're out in public," she explained. "Over top of the covering."

The bonnet felt hot and heavy and always about to slide off like a greasy spoon. You could almost forget the white mesh covering pinned lightly into the hair, but not the bonnet. Mama took one look at my askew bonnet with braids swinging below and decided Lancaster Mennonite Conference was far away. Dressing her girls appropriately for the trip could wait.

This time we crossed the ocean for the first time by airplane. It wasn't a jet, but on the way to becoming one. A "turbo prop"—half-propellor-half-jet. We made stops in Egypt, Israel, Italy, Switzerland, France, Germany, Holland, and England. Papa bought air tickets for nine of us, seven kids and two parents. Betty had already been in the U.S. for a year. I couldn't wait to see her, for us all to be together again. She'd help us know how to fit in.

The flights home began from Dira Dawa, Ethiopia. Papa had decided to visit the down-country stations of Dedar and Bedeno where the Mennonite Mission also had workers. Dedar's where we'd lived when we first came to Ethiopia. But I was just a toddler then. It was the home of my Horst and Gamber friends from boarding school. Their tales of impassible mud sloughs and treacherous mountain passes made our life in Nazareth seem tame. I'd been glad we didn't have to live down-country and only get to see our parents over Christmas and summer.

Papa made everything exciting. We may never have another chance to see these mountain villages and their patchwork farms quilting the hilltops. He hired a mule-train, and we four older children trekked deep into the countryside while Mama stayed in Dedar with the little boys. My mule insisted on leading the pack that dribbled along behind.

Then we were off the mules' backs and onto a bumpy flight to Addis Ababa. As the little passenger plane swam through the turbulent skies, I got airsick. Suddenly I didn't care if I lived down-country or in America. I only wanted to die. So what if we crashed? At least I'd be out of my misery. I closed my eyes and gagged, gagged again, but there was nothing, only bile and a spinning head.

My mule leads the pack.

I was sure I'd be too sick to travel to America. I never wanted to see another plane anyway. Give me a horse or mule any day. Or even an ocean liner. I'd never been this sick. Why did we have to travel by plane?

The next lap went better. In Egypt the customs man looked at all nine of us and our stacked luggage. "You just like Egyptians," he said grinning. "Many childrens."

Back in Lancaster we went to the Missionary Closet to find the ready-made cape dresses we'd need to attend Lancaster Mennonite School. You couldn't buy them in an ordinary store. If they didn't have our size in the Missionary Closet, we'd have to make the dresses or shop in a special store in downtown Lancaster that specialized in "plain attire."

Every time visitors from America had come, or I opened a birthday card from East Petersburg Mennonite Church or Morris Run Mennonite Church, I'd known we were part of a people, a Mennonite people. We were different from the Ethiopians, and we were different from the Sudan Interior Mission, Lutheran, Presbyterian, and Baptist missionaries.

Now we'd be trying to fit in with our people. Those lovely ladies from East Petersburg Mennonite Church sewing circle who had made dresses for me, had even sewed frilly lace on the collar and sleeves of my navy-blue dress. I liked looking fancier than my sisters.

There'd be different foods too. Once in Ethiopia a package had arrived for Mama, filled with delicacies she loved but couldn't get in Ethiopia—Lebanon Bologna and chocolate chips. Things I'd never heard of.

We all wanted a taste. Of course. But the package had been weeks in the hold of a hot cargo ship. and the food emerged from the package totally inedible—permeated with the strong flavor of moth balls that seeped from the clothing in the rest of the package. The chocolate chips had melted into one big, foul-smelling blob.

"I'll keep in touch," I promised Ethiopian friends as we left, but I didn't do very well. Ethiopia was home if my family was there. Now we had left.

Mama's brother, Uncle Samuel, had bought us a big yellow station wagon. The mission board had a home ready for us in East Petersburg, near the church of the Sunday School class that always sent me birthday cards and dresses with lacy collars. East Petersburg is also where real Lebanon Bologna and chocolate chips came from. And sandwiches of strange, sharp-tasting Swiss cheese. The first time I tasted it, I spit out my sandwich. All of us kids did until Mama turned to us, her big brown eyes shining reproachfully behind her glasses.

"Children, this cheese is special! Our family used to sell Swiss cheese and lots of other kinds at the Lancaster Farmers' Market. It's delicious! I haven't tasted any for six years. I'll eat your sandwich if you don't want it!" She took a big bite from my sandwich.

Every Sunday morning and evening we'd visit different Mennonite churches around Lancaster. Sometimes Papa would preach and sometimes we'd all stand up and sing, *"There were ninety and nine that safely lay in the shelter of the fold. But one was out on the hills away, far off from the gates of gold..."*

As we sang about the lost sheep wandering on the mountain side, I'd give my little brother a quick elbow in the ribs and he'd "baa" at the right times. The people loved it! They weren't used to seeing a whole missionary family of eight kids all standing up singing. Sunday evening church was when we usually sang missionary songs and told missionary stories.

I made up a little skit about a time we went camping at Lake Hawassa and some of the men saw a leopard, but they didn't tell us kids until the end of the week because they didn't want us to be scared.

Our life in Ethiopia had been so different from what most Mennonites knew.

The Wenger family.

They went deep-sea fishing, but at Lake Hawassa, we caught cat-fish. The biggest was 32" long. Twelve-inchers were so little we'd throw them back. And we didn't have professional cleaners. Papa would nail the fish right through the gills to a tree. Then he'd slice the thin gray skin around the top, grab the top edge with a pliers and peel it off like it was a banana.

They had Bible quizzing, but at Lake Hawasa we'd sit on logs around a campfire telling stories and playing Bible quiz games. Papa tried to come up with really hard questions for us older kids—like what were the Hebrew names of Shadrach, Meshach and Abednego? Or Moses' mother? Or the names of the magicians that tried to stump Moses? Or the people that walked with Jesus on the Emmaus Road?

People seemed freer to laugh in Sunday evening church, but on Sunday mornings Lancaster Mennonites were more quiet. They didn't move much or show if they were happy or sad. They'd all stand to sing two hymns after the song leader found the right note on the pitch pipe. He'd beat time to keep us on track. I sang soprano, but Margaret knew how to sing alto. I tried too, but the melody was easier. Papa sang bass. After that we'd all turn around and kneel by the wooden benches while the leader prayed.

Our preachers wore stiff black or gray plain suits--"straight cuts" we called them. They were special Mennonite suits without lapels and flashy neck ties like worldly people wore. Papa used to wear a straight cut. All the men did. That kept us different from the world like God said. We should be, "nonconformed." We'd hear that a lot. That's why we didn't have pianos or televisions either.

I remembered how I felt at Bingham—long braids, a covering. We were just kids, but we still felt different, like we didn't fit in. But being in Ethiopia must have changed us. Over there no one had ever heard of Mennonites. They didn't know what those white things were on our heads and why we never cut our hair or wore sleeveless dresses or jewelry and make-up. And why our men wore straight cuts.

And it wasn't only the other missionaries, it was the Ethiopians. People would ask Papa if that special coat meant he was a Catholic father. Of course he couldn't be a priest with all us kids, but who was he? The Ethiopians didn't like Catholics because Ethiopians were Coptic

Orthodox, and they didn't need Catholics. Or maybe he was a communist?

Papa didn't like all the questions from the Ethiopians, so he started wearing a different coat and even a tie when he went to the government offices on official business for the mission. But then people from the mission board came for a visit, and he got in trouble. He didn't wear his plain suit to the airport to meet the mission leaders. He'd sent a letter to explain the reason for his change, but they didn't read the letter before they saw him.

Talk about shock. He was being disloyal, breaking his promise to the church. We were sent to Ethiopia by people wearing plain suits and coverings so we shouldn't be breaking those standards if we wanted to be part of the group. And I did. These were my people. I wasn't an SIMer. I wasn't an Ethiopian. I was a Mennonite. So if I had to put up my long braids and fit them under a covering, I'd do it. I wanted to fit in somewhere.

But it was a struggle each morning, getting my long hair up. The hair pins poked my head and if I was late for class and had to run, my sloppy bun shook and sagged all day. And I hated wearing stockings and the girdles to hold them up. The stockings had to be gray or black or have seams up the back so your legs didn't look naked. It took a long time to get dressed each morning.

And shoes? I wore sneakers if I had to wear something. But for school I bought slip-ons with wedge heels like Mama and the other missionary women wore.

One Sunday we visited a big Mennonite church near the EMM offices in Salunga. Papa was preaching, and then we had communion. It took a long time for all of us to get the bread and grape juice, then all the women went to the basement to wash feet with each other.

We'd washed feet with our little Ethiopia mission team, but now with hundreds of Mennonites? I followed the other women to the basement where I got paired with an older woman.

I watched as she reached up and unhooked the black stockings from her girdle. This was definitely more complicated than when I'd run around in bare feet. I hated wearing stockings, but, oh well, that's how it was done here.

Feet bared, she sat in the chair beside the basin first. She looked so somber. Everyone did. She never smiled or said a word even when I splashed handfuls of warm water over her white foot. Crease marks streaked along the edges of the feet so recently released from their stocking-shoe prison. Water dropped on the towel I'd hurriedly flung over my lap.

Then it was my turn. I sat in the chair while my partner took the towel from me. Wordlessly she showed me it was really an apron, a towel apron. In a quiet, exaggerated fashion she tied the apron strings around her waist, smoothed out the towel, and stooped to wash my feet. I looked down on her reddish gray-streaked hair and flushed with shame. I'd done it all wrong!

Usually I loved school and church when we'd all be together, the men on one side and the women on the other. I was old enough to sit up front with my youth on the women's side, of course. The little kids sat in back with their parents. The ministers, Brother Landis or Brother Weaver, would read from the Bible and then talk about it. Mostly it was boring, but I liked seeing my friends and learning how church worked here in America.

Some of the people who smiled at our "missionary stories" thought missionaries shouldn't have so many children. All those boat and plane tickets to get us where we needed to go—and then the special boarding schools to help us get a good education.

Once Mama said she sort of apologized to the mission leader. But he just smiled and said, "The more children, the more missionaries." I liked that. And I decided to try to keep that rally going.

We got outfitted with capes and coverings so we could go to Lancaster Mennonite School. Margaret and I were in 10th grade. Kids were friendly. "Your parents are missionaries?" they asked, wide-eyed. They liked hearing about the leopards, the pythons, hippos, crocodiles, and hyenas.

"Yeah," I'd shrug. And always felt like adding, "Aren't yours? Isn't that what we're all supposed to be doing?" I felt like our family was really obeying God to go to "the ends of the earth." Didn't Jesus tell his disciples right before he left, "Go into all the world and preach..." Not just stay in Lancaster, build big, beautiful houses—and get rich growing tobacco and driving fast cars?

I couldn't believe how important cars were to the guys in my class. Spending all their money to get the latest model. We hadn't even owned a car in Ethiopia—just used an old van or truck that belonged to the mission. And our furniture? We made a couch out of an old army cot. We leaned pillows against the wall for a back. All four of us girls slept in one room—in two metal frame bunk beds. And our house was so leaky that dust blew in under the door.

Right before we left Ethiopia, we gave some of our old clothes to a neighbor family. The man worked as a watchman for the Academy.

It made me feel funny to see his little girl wearing my old gray plaid dress. We were going to throw it away because I'd torn the skirt on a thorn bush. But she smiled shyly at me, so proud of her new dress. And then our old tin cans. The watchman found them in our garbage bin and asked if he could have them. They were great for storing oil or dipping out water.

Were we rich? Well, in Ethiopia it sure felt like we were. But here in America? Maybe if people didn't spend so much money on houses and cars, we could send more missionaries or help the Ethiopians more. I wanted to obey. And I wanted to belong to a group of people that obeyed Jesus too—even with the hard stuff.

I remember when an old missionary man who worked up along the Red Sea visited us at the Bible Academy. He'd worked in the desert with nomadic Muslims all his life. His skin was wrinkled and almost gray. He joined us for family worship one morning, and Papa invited him to lead.

He read a verse from Psalms 2, then pointed his bony finger at us. "Children, what do you want for your inheritance?"

Inheritance? I hardly knew what the word meant and certainly hadn't given it any thought. We all shrugged.

"Here in Psalm 2:8 God says, 'Ask of me and I will make the nations your inheritance, the ends of the earth your possession.' Let's pray that all together!"

And I did. Suddenly I knew that's how I wanted to spend my life. I wanted to go to the "nations," to see the "nations" follow Jesus.

11

Alone with the Mennonites

Mama and Papa talked a lot about whether or not they should go back to Ethiopia. It was 1963 by now. Betty was in college at Eastern Mennonite College, and Margaret and I were going into our junior year at LMS.

They'd take the other five kids along with them back to Ethiopia, but we three older girls would stay here. I'd liked Ethiopia, except for boarding school, but now I liked Lancaster too. I couldn't believe the sophomore class voted me in as secretary. People liked me? Did I belong?

Secretary was the most important girl job in the school. Two boys for president and vice-president; two girls for secretary and treasurer. We'd meet to plan special class events—service projects like singing at the Millersville Children's Home or rolling bandages for MCC. And socials—ice-skating parties, outdoor Flying Dutchman or Walk-a-Mile and indoor games.

I was full of ideas. I liked to talk. We were planning for refreshments after we sang at the Millersville Children's Home. Should it be popsicles or cups of ice cream? I voted for popsicles but everyone else wanted cups.

"But why?" I asked, incredulous. "Isn't it going to be a big mess and bother to scoop ice-cream into all those little cups?"

Brother Dietz, our class advisor, threw back his bushy-bearded head and guffawed loudly before turning his merry brown eyes on me.

"Miss Wenger, you grew up in Africa. I guess you don't know that we have prepacked ice cream in little cups with wooden spoons. We won't have to scoop it out."

"Oh." I said, deflated. More things to learn about America.

One morning I couldn't find the covering I usually wore for school. It must have gotten mashed between some textbooks, but I found another one just in time. I saw the matron eyeing me when I walked into chapel. It was Sister Wenger. I thought I'd like her because she'd been a missionary in Tanzania, but then her husband died of malaria. Died of malaria! That was scary. I'd had malaria too.

Anyhow, that made her a widow with three little children, so they came back to the U.S., and she got this job as the matron at LMS. She had a long nose and black glasses. Her hair was up in a big bun that stuck out the back of her head under a basket covering with strings to hold it on. Sister Wenger came to the study hall and said she wanted to talk with me.

I thought maybe we were gonna talk about Africa. I smiled. Then she took me to her office and asked me why I'd worn the covering I did that day. I clapped my hand on my head. "Oh, I couldn't find the other one. I was just glad I found this one so I could come to school."

She unpinned the covering and held it up to me. "Do you see that this front piece is only 1" wide? Our standards for a woman's covering explains that the front piece needs to be 1 ½" wide before the pleats begin."

I stared. I hadn't noticed the ½" difference. It covered my bun the same way.

She pinned the covering back on my head being careful to completely cover the bun. Then she sighed. "I'm sorry, but I'll have to give you a bad conduct grade for the semester because you broke the regulations."

She didn't even say anything about Africa! And now every day she stood there, her eagle eyes on me. Another day she pulled me aside. "Jewel, I can see your knees. That dress is too short. Please don't wear it to school again."

I flung my stack of textbooks on a nearby desk. My skirt fell full length covering my knees. "The books were just pulling it up," I retorted. "It covers my knees!"

Then we heard that the Supervising Committee of the school had decided that by next Monday, all girls' dresses had to fall three inches below the knees. This was Friday.

On Monday we tried to comply. One girl flaunted a long skirt with an obviously elongated fringe still showing the crease of the previous hem. Sister Wenger didn't look us in the eyes when we filed into chapel. Her eyes were on our hems.

I saw her pull Norma Jean out of the chapel line. Norma Jean? She was a senior, a studious girl, and spiritual, too. Not one of the rebellious ones who always tried to push the boundaries. Like Ruthie who balanced her tiny covering—it did have a big wide front piece—on her top knot that swept above her shapely neck. It did cover all her back hair, but in front there were rippling waves arranged around her face and side curls beside her ears.

Ruthie's hem had been ripped out over the weekend. It fell far below her well-tanned knees. Not Norma Jean's. She was expelled for the day—sent home to lengthen her skirts—or if there weren't ample hems, to get new modest dresses that met the requirements.

***

I loved drama. Not the skirt kind but the acting-out kind. When I was a little girl I told Papa I wanted to be an actress. He listened to me, but then said he hoped I'd find ways to use my gifts in the church. That would be better than being a movie star in Hollywood.

Our planning committee wrote several skits for the next school social and began practice. But then Brother Dietz told us the Supervising Committee had gone over the plans for our social and did not approve of skits. That was "play acting." It was too much like Hollywood—forcing you to act a lie, to pretend to be something or someone you weren't. Jesus said, "Let your yes be yes, and your no be no." No skits allowed. Choirs, quartets, or debate teams were okay, but not skits.

Really? I wanted to fit in, but was the box too small?

So I joined the Goodwill Singers and the debate team. Our debate topic was: "Resolved: Christians should not build bomb shelters." I thought we won, and everyone said we had the best arguments, but the judges handed it to the bomb shelter builders because we didn't prove "beyond a shadow of a doubt" that Christians should not sink precious resources—that could be going to support missions—into building bomb shelters in their back yards.

In the Goodwill Singers there was this boy who liked me. He'd always try to sit beside me when we went on bus tours. He was nice. Polite and friendly. Handsome too. He playfully snatched my copy of the program, and I thrilled that his hand brushed mine. But when I asked him what he wanted to do when he grew up, he said he was going to take over his parents' dairy farm. He never wanted to leave Lancaster County.

Never leave Lancaster County? I'd only been here two years. It was a nice enough place. Lots of Mennonites. My people. I'd look out over the annual Leadership Assembly—a sea of black plain suits and white mesh coverings over long buns of hair. I could fit in here easier than in Ethiopia. These are my people, I thought to myself. I'm fitting in.

Fitting in was like putting my hair up. Lots of tries, tears, and pricks from sharp hairpins. But finally, the hair all fit under the covering. I looked like everyone else.

But never leave? Never see yellow weaver birds plaiting nests in pink oleander hedges or shiver as hyenas howled into the night? Never get to swim across Lake Bishoftu, or drink fresh roast coffee brewed in a clay pot over a charcoal fire? Never see my old Ethiopian friends who might grow up and become church leaders?

If I could just get that boy to go to Africa. In fact if that whole assembly went, they'd know that Lancaster County was just one of many beautiful places. "Garden Spot of the World." True enough. But didn't Jesus say we should go to "the ends of the earth?"

My parents had gone back to Ethiopia with my five younger siblings in the summer of 1963. They planned to be gone for three years, so that's when we lived with Landis and Ruth Hershey and their two children, Betty Louise and Glen. They lived near LMS and attended Mellinger Mennonite.

Aunt Ruth, as we called her even though she wasn't a relative, was the sweetest, kindest lady you ever did meet. They took us right in like we were their own family. They also hosted other students from Ethiopia, like Ingida Asfaw, a young man from Dedar who went on to become a famous heart surgeon.

The summer after Margaret and I graduated from high school in 1965, we lived with the Hersheys and were working hard to save money for college the next year. That summer I got a strange phone call. It was Sister Wenger, the dean of women at LMS. She wondered if I'd like to come over for a cup of tea and a chat.

What? I was done with bad conduct grades for wearing the wrong size coverings. She didn't really care about me anyway, only the length of my skirts. What could she find wrong with me now? I'd written the words of the poem that had been chosen as the class song and Margaret had composed the tune. I'd been an editor for the school newspaper, *The Millstream.* Now I was off to college and not looking back.

"Thanks for the invitation," I told her coldly, "But I don't have time." I learned later she'd hated her job policing women's attire but didn't have many employment options. She was a widow with three children. Now I wish I'd drunk that cup of tea.

Betty, Margaret and Jewel on the steps
of Landis and Ruth Hershey's home
during the years the rest of our family
was in Ethiopia.

Part 2

12

Off to College

The David and Rhoda Showalter family at the time Richard and Jewel met.

I didn't have a hard time deciding where to go to college. Eastern Mennonite College was four hours away in Virginia, but that's where Papa and Mama had gone, and that's where Betty was. It was a place where I could fit in. Maybe. Not many from Lancaster were going away to college. That boy who liked me—he was only too glad to stop the books and start the milking.

I'd been dating a guy I liked when we went away to college. He came to college too, but we decided to break up because of all the other young adults we'd be meeting.

Then there was this other family on campus, David and Rhoda Showalter. They had been friends with my parents and even came to New York City to see us off to Ethiopia for the first time we left back in 1949 when I was one year old. David and his oldest son, Richard, were both students at EMC during my freshman year.

One day Rhoda Showalter called the dorm and invited my two older sisters and me for supper. They lived just on the other side of the hill behind the campus, so we hiked up. I liked how their family was a lot like ours—except they had three boys first while we had three girls. Their two little boys, Jonnie and Joe, reminded me of my little brothers, Phil and Tommy. While we'd been in Ethiopia they'd been in southeastern Kentucky planting two churches back in the hills.

Then one day I got a call from Richard Showalter. I barely knew him. He was the oldest in that Showalter family, and I'd passed him on the sidewalk a few times. He asked me to go to a concert with him. Then we went to a movie. I could tell he really liked me. I went on a picnic with his family. We hiked up Massanutten Peak at dawn, and he brought along a thermos of hot golden rod tea he'd made.

He was different from the Lancaster County guys I'd dated. He was quiet, almost shy, but loved to talk about deep things—like why it was hard for Kentucky people to become Mennonites. I liked the way he thought and his original ideas. He also wore a plain suit. Most young Mennonite men I knew weren't wearing those old-fashioned suits anymore. When he asked me to go to the spring banquet with him and bought me a gorgeous yellow rose corsage, I was afraid he'd wear his dreadful black plain suit. And he did.

One day as we sipped chocolate milkshakes, he asked me if we could "go steady." That scared me. I was only 17, and I wasn't sure what I wanted in a husband. I knew I didn't fit in, really, even though I was trying. He didn't fit in either. And going with him didn't help me fit in.

A friend told me Richard's second cousin was a quarterback on the high school football team, and we went to watch them play. I couldn't figure out what was going on. I'd never seen such a silly game before. Something else I'd have to learn if I became a real American.

Now the other kind of football, or soccer, as they called it in America, was something I loved. We used to play soccer in Ethiopia. Anywhere. Barefoot on the beach at Lake Hawasa, we three older girls against Papa and Chet. Or on the hospital compound, just a couple kids with a ball and goal post stones.

Here at EMC we started playing soccer in physical education mostly just to learn the rules. It was a new game for everyone. One day I ran down the field and headed the ball into a goal. Miss Martin, the teacher, cheered and clapped her hands.

"Girls," she yelled. "Jewel knows how to play soccer. She grew up in Ethiopia. Look. She just showed you how to head the ball! No hands allowed, but you can use your head."

Maybe it was okay not to fit in? Richard didn't seem to care if he fit in.

***

After my first year of college, Richard took me back to the Hersheys in Lancaster before he headed to Ohio. The Hersheys were our second family. When they knew we were coming to live with them, they had even built a new bedroom over their garage so they had room for the three "Wenger girls."

We helped them out a little with cleaning and cooking each week, but mostly they just loved and included us in their family. They said they'd always wanted to have more children and had lost a little girl who was born handicapped. They had one girl older than we were and one younger boy, so we fit right in between.

Margaret and I always fought over the household chores in the Hershey household because we both liked cooking better than cleaning. The first person downstairs on Saturday mornings got to pick. I usually got down first.

One Saturday, though, Margaret beat me downstairs, so I was stuck with the cleaning. She was gloating. When I went out on the balcony to shake my dust rag, she locked the door behind me. That way she could get her work done and I'd still be slaving away.

If I banged on the door, Aunt Ruth would come running and we'd both be in trouble. I wondered if I could jump from the balcony. Clenching the dust rag in my teeth, I swung my leg over the banister, hung from the edge of the balcony with both hands and dropped to the lawn below. It was a jolt, but no sprained ankles. I dusted myself off and walked calmly into the kitchen. Margaret was at the sink with her back to the door. She turned just in time to catch my innocent smile as I headed upstairs to finish the dusting.

Richard planned to spend the summer drywalling in Ohio, where his parents had recently moved. I planned to work at Martins Meats. Hersheys owned Martins Meats so they were glad to give us work. We could walk down to the plant from their home, but you had to dress for it. The whole place was refrigerated. People were talkative and friendly. We stuffed hot dogs in five-pound boxes or vac-packed them into one pounders as they flew past on the assembly line.

I liked living at the Hersheys, but this was the last summer we'd be there. Next summer our family was coming home from Ethiopia. Hersheys' two-story brick home stood along the Old Philadelphia Pike. This is where Richard would drop me after my first year of college.

He turned in the drive. It was early afternoon, and he still had to drive all the way to Ohio. We wouldn't see each other every day like we had at college. I could tell he was nervous. We had to make some kind of decision about our relationship.

He looked sideways at me so he could hear better. Ever since he'd had a serious mastoid ear infection as a child he was hard of hearing in his right ear. That made conversation in the car more difficult.

"Would it be okay if I came to see you this summer or if we write letters?" he asked tentatively. He was so good at reading people. That's one thing I liked about him, his sensitivity. He knew I wasn't all in on the friendship like he was. He didn't want to push too hard.

I was trying to make up my mind, too. I liked him, but was he really the man I wanted to marry? I couldn't bring myself to reject his offer though.

"Okay," I said. "Let's try writing letters."

He carried my suitcase in, then turned to go. I waved him off, glad to be rid of boy thoughts for a while.

A week later a letter came from Richard. "Missing you," he said. Drywall work was slack. It looked like he wasn't going to be able to earn as much money as he'd hoped. His parents had built a new home in Plain City and were working at Rosedale Bible College.

As I read the letter I felt tired and uncertain. Each week at college I'd thought I'd break up with him. I didn't want to string him along, but each time we parted I couldn't bring myself to hurt him. He was so nice. He really liked me. There was something so stalwart, deep, unique and precious. We were different from each other. I was outgoing and talkative, wanting to be popular and fit in. He was reserved and serious. He didn't seem to care about fitting in. He didn't mind wearing a plain suit in the winter or sandals in the summer even if everyone else was wearing lapel suits with ties and dress shoes. He lived by his convictions.

I started writing a letter in reply, struggling with what to say. Now that he was gone, I was sure we were too different. It would never work. There was still plenty of time to date around. He was three years older than I was. So I wrote him a "Dear John" letter and ended things. I told him I didn't feel I could give any more of myself to him. I didn't see any future in our relationship and didn't want to take time just writing letters as "pen pals."

It was cowardly, I know. But I thought it might soften the blow. He was so nice I didn't want to hurt him more than I had to. The next year I planned to live with my family and attend Millersville University so Richard and I wouldn't be seeing each other every day.

When my family returned from Ethiopia, Papa took a job working for Eastern Mennonite Missions as director of Home Ministries. Mama and the rest of the kids had to learn how to live in America all under one roof. I commuted to Millersville University and fielded questions from family about life in America as though I were an expert and really did fit in.

I missed my EMC friends and the dorm comaraderie. I dated a couple other local guys and heard that Richard dated several other girls. One friend wrote to say I needed to come back and "rescue Richard" from these dates she didn't approve of.

Then I got a card from Richard. He was part of a study tour to Eastern Europe and wrote about the beauty of Prague. He said he hoped I could see it someday. He called it "the most beautiful city in the world." Then he asked me if I would be willing to serve as feature editor of the college newspaper, the *Weather Vane*, next year. He'd been named editor and was pulling his staff together.

By now I was starting to miss Richard and the conversations we'd had. Other guys seemed shallow. When I asked Papa for advice he said if a girl had treated him like I'd treated Richard he didn't think he'd ever go back. Maybe I'd lost my opportunity.

Back at EMC in the fall of 1967 I joined Richard and other staffers in the *Weather Vane* office. I loved how he chaired the meetings and commented in class. We were both English majors. But he was also majoring in history and Bible.

How could I let him know I was open to exploring a special friendship again? A full-page magazine ad for Johnnie Walker whisky caught my eye. "I'm waiting for a Kentucky gentleman. How about you?" an attractive blonde asked.

When no one was around I clipped the ad from the magazine and pinned it on the bulletin board in the *WV* office. No one ever found out it was me.

Then as I studied in the library one afternoon, Richard slid in beside me. "Could I see you out in the hall on some non-*Weather Vane* business?" he asked.

I followed him out and there in the hall he asked if I'd be interested in hiking Laird's Knob that Saturday. It would be a double date with my sister Betty and her fiancé Nelson Good who was a friend of Richard's.

I said yes and knew immediately that this time I was all in. We never ran out of things to talk about. We'd often get so engrossed in conversation that he'd get me back to the dorm after the curfew since he refused to wear a watch and be bothered about time. Later he bought me a necklace watch so we could keep better track of the time.

After Christmas in Ohio with his family we got engaged on New Year's Eve sitting on the office couch at my home in Pennsylvania. We'd just driven eight hours from his home in Plain City, Ohio. Travel weary yet loathe to say good night.

"Will you be mine?" he whispered, his arm draped around my shoulder. Had I heard him right? Was this a proposal? I didn't think he'd ask me this soon. We'd only been dating four months this time round. Was I ready to commit my life to him forever? I was only 19. Other men I knew were more dashing, more handsome, but none were kinder or deeper. He loved me passionately, and I was beginning to love him. He'd won my heart.

"Yes," I said, my eyes shining with tears of joy and fear. We kissed for the first time.

That night an icy rain fell coating every pine needle, branch, and twig in sight. I didn't need a diamond. Thousands sparkled from every bush. The rising sun turned the world into the most beautiful diadem as we drove to his cousin's wedding then returned for Christmas with my family.

Time sped up. We thought we'd marry when I graduated from college a year and a half later, but then Richard won a Rockefeller Fellowship and made plans to enter the divinity school at the University of Chicago. He wasn't at EMC anymore.

The draft flung young men our age at the Vietnam War—or something alternative, since we were Mennonite conscientious objectors to war. Richard took a job working for Rosedale Mennonite Missions as Assistant Service Director.

This had him on the road, overseeing the work of voluntary service units in Jackson, Mississippi, Cincinnati, Ohio, Louisville, Kentucky, Flint, Michigan, and El Dorado, Arkansas. He taught winter term at Rosedale Bible College and led Mission Service weekends for young people all over conference from New York to Kansas.

We wrote letters daily, pouring out our differing experiences and thoughts, longing for the time when there would only be occasional "spaces in our togetherness" rather than what was now only short times of "togetherness in our spaces."

As our months apart lengthened and Richard made plans to move to Chicago, he urged me to go with him. Why wait until my graduation in the spring of 1969? Now that we'd decided to share our lives, why not invest more in our "reservoir of common experiences?"

My parents did not feel good about me dropping out of college to get married. In a long phone call one evening they almost insisted that I finish college before marriage. I couldn't just expect a man to take care of me all my life. I should think more about my own schooling and future career options.

I sobbed into the phone, feeling pulled between the man I loved and our plans together and my own desire to finish college and please my parents. We wrote, talked, cried, prayed, and reasoned, rolling our wedding date back from June 1969 to December 1968 and finally settling on September 14, 1968.

We honeymooned in Belleville, Pennsylvania, while Richard also finished writing a Sunday school quarterly and led a Mission Service weekend—commitments already in the works before we'd moved our wedding date up. Then with Richard's little Rambler packed with clothes and wedding gifts we moved to Chicago together.

Our marriage September 14, 1968.

Our first home was a furnished efficiency apartment on the tenth floor of married-student housing at 5110 Kenwood Street on Chicago's southside. While Richard plunged into studies in the divinity school, I worked in the university library and took classes in the English department to transfer back to EMC where I was completing my BA in English.

We began visiting Mennonite churches in the city—first Woodlawn, an African American church near the university. But after several Sundays we felt almost scared and strangely unwelcome. The black power movement was gaining strength, and the oil of our white Mennonite identity and university enrollment did not mix well with the water of the black south side.

Later we found a home at Lawndale Mennonite, an Hispanic congregation in the northwest of the city. We were warmly welcomed to the English service of the bilingual congregation.

On many weekends and holidays we were back in Mennonite churches in Illinois, Indiana, Iowa, or Ohio to speak with youth about mission and service opportunities. Richard began leading meetings on spiritual renewal even though he was not an ordained pastor. We attended Mennonite mission meetings in Chicago that brought together leaders from across the church for the Council of International Anabaptist Ministries.

We loved the church and wanted to serve God. Mark Peachey, Richard's boss at RMM, proposed that he be licensed for his growing public preaching and teaching ministry. We travelled to Richard's childhood home on Buckhorn Creek in Kentucky for the licensing service. Mark also asked me to speak. Sometimes we spoke together at youth retreats, or he'd preach, and I'd lead a children's meeting.

After one year in Chicago, we led a servanthood work camp for Mennonite youth in Jackson, Mississippi. I'd never cooked much before marriage and now fumbled along preparing meals for the whole camp. I read the recipes meticulously, learning the names of strange ingredients to follow the menu plans laid out by the unit leader.

Richard and I slept together on a double mattress on the floor of the Voluntary Service unit hall closed off by a curtain. A box fan stirred the damp night air. I'd never been so hot. As soon as the camp was over I flew to Virginia to take my last summer school college classes at EMC. Neither one of us looked forward to a summer of separation, but the compromise had allowed us to move to Chicago together. Richard continued his itinerant administrative work for RMM, visiting young adults in Voluntary Service units from Arkansas to Kentucky.

In Chicago I'd decided not to wear my Mennonite covering. I still wore my hair long and uncut—fitting in well with the free-flowing hippie styles of the times. But whenever we went to Mennonite churches in Ohio or Indiana, I donned a covering.

That summer in Mississippi I wore my Mennonite covering. We were leading the camp, holding up the ideal. The young people who came were from Kalona, Iowa. It was their first time in this large, southern city.

After a hot day repainting the flaking wood siding of the Voluntary Service unit house, we took off for an outing in an amusement park. I stood at the bottom of a large, swooping slide while the workcamp youth group clambered up and screamed down dozens of times.

I noticed a cluster of bystanders watching these Mennonite girls from Iowa. One sidled up, smiling. She addressed a dark-haired Iowa girl who was just smoothing down her lavender flowered shirtwaist dress that had billowed up around her on the downward plunge.

"Why do you wear those white things on your heads?" the Jackson lady asked.

"Oh," said the Iowa girl. "We're Mennonites. This is how Mennonites dress." And she left to dash up the stairs for another trip down the slide.

There was nothing complicated or theological about her answer. No reference to I Corinthians 11, God's order of creation and prayer veilings for modest women who wanted to please God.

So maybe our unique Mennonite clothing—all the things Sister Wenger had tried so hard to enforce back at LMS—was nothing more than our "tribal" attire? God didn't really command this in the Bible? But our leaders had decided this is how they knew who was faithful. And if I wanted to fit in, to be part of the group, that was a small price to pay.

In Virginia for summer school I lived with my mother's parents, Lloyd and Sara Weaver. They'd recently retired to Harrisonburg after years in Newport News, Virginia, where they'd worked in friendly outreach to the oriental sailors whose ships idled in the Norfolk and Newport News harbors. (See Appendix A)

Jewel's maternal grandparents, Lloyd and Sara Weaver.

I'd always loved my Grandma Weaver. During the Christmas breaks we spent with them she'd tell us stories of their work along the docks. She and Grandpa played Scrabble at every meal, and they taught me special Scrabble words. It seemed I could talk to her about anything.

She told me that years ago she had vowed she'd never eat breakfast but would spend that time praying for her family. Her three sons were all working for the church, and her one daughter, my mom, was a missionary. She had prayed for her husband when he loved sports more than he loved God. He had never even prayed out loud in public before they got married, but then he became a preacher and still loved to play golf.

She told me she was always real shy and never wanted to speak in public or teach a Sunday school class. But when she and Grandpa really gave their lives to God, she told God she'd do anything he wanted her to do. Soon she got asked to teach a class, and she couldn't say no. She became one of the best teachers around.

"Your grandma was my favorite teacher," an elderly woman told me years later. "She really loved us, and she knew her Bible."

I loved how Grandma made God a part of her life every day. It just seemed natural. One day I was helping her can pears, and every time a jar pinged with a seal, she squealed with joy, "Thank you, God!"

She told me once she was travelling on a bus down to the Newport News dock, and she struck up a friendly conversation with the man sitting beside her. He was a retired truck driver. Then he asked her what she did, and she said, "I'm a fisher of men!"

Now that's what Jesus had said to some of his disciples when he called them to drop their nets and come follow him. But when Grandma said that to the strange man beside her on the bus, he just looked all shocked and uncomfortable.

She tried to explain what Jesus meant, but I'm sure he thought she was a crazy religious weirdo instead of a sweet, little old Grandma. We both laughed, and then I started wondering if that's where the term "hooker" came from—if some women really were "fishing for men!"

Anyway, Grandma and I had fun talking with each other. God was woven through her whole life, not just tacked on. I told her I wanted to interview her for a paper I was writing for Mennonite history.

I asked her about her childhood, growing up on a farm in Lititz, and how she and Grandpa met. I asked her how long they'd been married before my mom came along.

Suddenly Grandma got real quiet. She looked down, thinking hard, then she looked me straight in the eye. "Jewel, I've never told anyone the answer to that question, and I don't think I will now. Let's go on to your other questions."

"Sure, Grandma," I said, but I knew there was more to that story. Later I asked my mom. "Yes," she said. "My parents had to get married. I was already on the way." She looked down too. This was a family secret I'd stumbled on.

"My mother never told me either," she said. "But I saw the date of my parents' marriage and my birth in the family Bible."

All those plain suits and capes covered over hearts that could be just as greedy and impatient as other people's hearts. Mennonites work at following the way of Jesus, living holy lives, doing hard stuff like loving your enemies, but it takes more than plain clothes and coverings. Is it helpful to have those visible, inlaid reminders that we're called to live lives conformed to Christ and not the world? And then we all help keep each other accountable?

After two years in Chicago and an MTh for Richard, we decided to take jobs back at Eastern Mennonite College. President Myron Augsburger invited Richard to serve as his assistant while also teaching in the Bible & Philosophy Department. The college offered me work as assistant director of communications.

This seemed like the right next step. Some of our younger siblings were coming to the college. Myron was someone we looked up to, a well-known evangelist and leader in the broader Mennonite church.

13

First Real Jobs

We spent the summer in Rosedale working for the mission board. That's when we found out I was pregnant. I was 23 and not quite sure I was ready for this new chapter, but Richard was over-the-moon excited. And this would be the first grandchild on both sides of the family. We took his parents, David and Rhoda Showalter, out for supper and told them they were going to be grandparents.

We made plans to rent a little two-bedroom house that had grown out of a remodeled garage on South College Avenue in Harrisonburg, Virginia. It had a large yard and was located south of the college, but within easy walking distance. We scrounged together simple furnishings from a thrift store and unpacked some of our wedding gifts for the first time.

Chester David, officially nicknamed "Chad" joined us on March 24, 1971. I worked for one semester but resigned before his birth. I never considered working when I had a baby to care for. Why wouldn't I want to care for my own child?

Early wave feminism was influencing the culture and the role of women. I felt pressure to be "more than a housewife," especially in the academic environment of a college town. Chad seemed to understand

133

my frequent temptations to focus on something other than him and his wishes.

I enrolled in a graduate program in English at James Madison University and did some freelance writing. Two years after Chad's birth, Ella Mae Miller, a popular women's speaker on Mennonite Hour's *Heart to Heart* program, stopped in to ask me about writing and voicing several scripts. I was eager to explore other jobs and interests, but during her visit, Chad demanded she leave and held up a book insisting that I read to him even though I'd read non-stop most of the morning.

Jewel holding baby Chad with her mother-in-law Rhoda Showalter and Rhoda's mother, Amelia Swartzentruber.

I was filled with love and rage for this child tyrant. How could he hold such power over me?

Thoroughly embarrassed by his behavior and not knowing what to do, I sent him to the next room so we could finish our conversation. He ran from the room, squatted in a corner and deliberately pooped in his pants even though he had been potty trained.

I didn't know how to handle this and was loathe to punish him. Hadn't I been punished unfairly at boarding school with the strap? Mrs. Wallace had once made me lie to stop a beating. I wasn't going to do that to my child! Did he really poop his pants on purpose, or maybe he had to go really bad, and I was neglecting him to talk to my friend?

And then there was the time I was trying to complete work for my English graduate course. Chad woke unexpectedly from his usual three-hour nap. He was teething. But it was a time slot I'd intended to use for writing my research paper. Other days he'd wake early and cry unconsolably when I was just trying to take a shower in peace.

And why wasn't my husband helping me more? One night we lay in bed arguing about who would get up with the baby. "Can't you do it? I don't feel well," I begged, suffering from a bout of mastitis. Richard said he wished he could, but he had to teach in the morning.

I had never thought of myself as a selfish person. I'd grown up with seven siblings—plenty of spats and sibling rivalries, but this was a new challenge. In my frustration and anger, I turned to God and began to grow in new ways. Is this what Jesus meant when he called us to deny ourselves, to "take up our crosses?" Could I not learn to lay down my life in new ways for a helpless child who had not asked to be born?

I'd read about the test tube babies in *A Brave New World* where the terms "mother" and "father" were being erased from the language as something old fashioned, dirty, and obscene.

"Don't you think we should try to split things more 50/50?" I argued with Richard on one particularly frustrating day of childrearing.

He countered that it's all about seasons of life, that we couldn't artificially split up each day. In this season I was doing things for Chad he couldn't do, but that later in life there'd often be seasons when he'd spend more time with Chad—going out for lunch, hunting, or shoot-ing baskets.

And that's exactly the way it was. I saw the wisdom in his words. Each child thrives with a mother and a father who are committed to each other and to him/her throughout every season of life. Neither mother nor father is pursuing first and foremost their own goals and career without thought of how those decisions affect their spouse and children.

Marriage is not about a contract, it's a covenant. What's mine is yours; what's yours is mine. Fully and unreservedly. A partnership, a complimentary relationship. Like C.S. Lewis said, "It's more like a dance than a drill" or I might add, a tally sheet.

There are higher goals to be served—an eternal Kingdom of God that we're called to "seek first." On one level I'd known this all my life, but now I started to understand more personally my larger calling and purpose. We'd lay down our lives for this child and any others the Lord might give us. We'd love, honor, and lay down our lives for each other in our marriage. This was home. This was belonging.

About a month before Chad was born, Richard had been planning to attend a rare leadership conference led by Francis Schaeffer several hours away. I didn't want him to go and was afraid to stay by myself this close to the delivery. What if the baby came early? Fears crowded my mind. But Richard left for the conference, and I resigned myself to staying alone for the weekend.

Several hours later I heard the door open and Richard walked in. Stunned, I ran to embrace him. "What happened?" I asked. He said that God hadn't given him peace to leave me alone, and that loving his wife was more important than attending a conference. I'd never felt more loved.

When Chad was five months old, we moved into an intentional community named *Middle Earth* on the edge of campus—with 12 students, seven guys and five girls. Students were advocating for greater freedom between the sexes than the men's and women's dorms afforded. Hippie communes offered love and community. Why couldn't we experience this at our Mennonite college? We believed in Christian community. The early church shared lives, finances, and food. Why shouldn't we?

President Augsburger wanted to respond to students' requests but maintain community standards that did not give in to the "free love," drugs, and drinking of a hippie commune. He'd consider allowing male and female students to live together in an intentional community if there were a faculty couple present. Students signed a covenant stating that they would abide by school standards.

We pooled funds and took turns cooking dinner each night. We heard each other's stories over shared dinners and family meetings. We learned of the pain that many carried—divorced parents, estrangement, abandonment, trauma from accidents. Everyone seemed so lost, confused, and hungry for love and meaning.

In *Middle Earth* Richard and I had two rooms of our own—a bedroom we shared with Chad and a sitting room/office dubbed "Lothlorien" of the elvan kingdom. Our *Middle Earth* group living/dining room was "The Shire." Several couples formed and began spending lots of time together. We held a retreat to talk about our relationships with each other.

At first I wondered if we were just overseeing a group of campus rebels wanting to push the boundaries. Most had grown up in Christian homes but were far from committed Christians. It couldn't have been called a "Discipleship House."

One artistic student carpeted the living room with a patchwork of leftover carpet scraps. In this no-furniture room we'd sit cross-legged. Wandering hippies dropped in. We held open discussions/seminars on books like B.F. Skinner's *Walden Two*, and the behaviorism that shaped his utopian community.

One day a big white turkey showed up on the lawn. It must have escaped from a nearby turkey farm. We called it "food from heaven" and took great delight in butchering it for a communal meal, chopping off its head, gutting it, and plucking off the feathers.

EMU students watch as Richard butchers a turkey for the Middle Earthlings to eat.

Around 2 am one night we heard a knock on the door of Lothlorien. A student asked if we could join the group of Middle Earthlings all sitting on the living room floor. Some were crying. Someone said there was a crisis. They really were lost and needed help. They wanted to be "saved."

We spent the rest of the night talking about God, pulling out Bibles and praying as students wept and confessed disappointments and sins. Most said they wanted a fresh start. What did it mean to follow God? They at least wanted to try.

By now it was spring. It was not unusual to see students head off on cycles with Bibles tucked in their backpacks or sprawled on the lawn to read and pray together.

This experience made us long for deeper community with some of our peers, so the following year we helped to form Gemeinschaft that included two other young married couples and an eclectic group of singles who were part of the community for all or part of the year.

Besides his work teaching, Richard began to get frequent invitations to lead renewal meetings in Mennonite churches far from Virginia. He'd come home excited about the way God was touching lives, transforming congregations, but I felt left out, trapped at home with a demanding child.

Richard was a good listener. He heard my feelings, and we talked of ways to be involved together. We decided that whenever possible, we'd all go as a family. One weekend trip to upstate New York wouldn't give time to drive. I was touched when Richard booked flights for all of us. Family togetherness was costly but deeply valued.

I loved being included, but the travel stretched little Chad. Knowing that we were welcome, even when it cost extra money and disruption, gave a new feeling of peace. Now I sometimes opted to stay home. Just knowing we were always welcome brought peace and security.

During this season I turned from writing research papers for an MA in English to writing children's literature. Chad loved the nonsensical jingles of Nursery Rhymes, and one day as he endlessly chanted, "Barber, barber, shave a pig. How many hairs can make a wig?" I thought to myself, why not have him chanting something more worthwhile, and Biblical Nursery Rhymes were born. (See Appendix B)

Mary, Mary, Virgin Mary
How does your Jesus grow?
With stature tall and love for all
God's people here below.

***

Isaac loved Esau;
Rebecca loved Jacob;
And that was the reason
They couldn't make-up!

***

Wee little Zachee
Climbed up a tree
Up a wall, up a tree
Anything to see
Straining to see Jesus
Sighting o'er the throng
If I've cheated anyone
Four times I will repay

***

By now I was pregnant with our second child, and we were sensing it was time for a change. We did not feel drawn to invest in the university setting long-term. Richard spent a week in fasting and prayer. Numerous offers and invitations came for mission or other church vocation opportunities.

Richard met Paul Kraybill, the general secretary of Eastern Mennonite Missions, an organization that felt like family to me. They'd sent us to Ethiopia in 1949 when I was one year old. They'd visited us and overseen the fledgling schools, hospitals, and church that were taking shape in Ethiopia. And now that the overseas phase of life was over for the Wenger family, Papa had taken a job in their home office.

Paul Kraybill had visited us in Ethiopia. He helped organize the work of the missionaries and their needs. We didn't have to go around raising funds like a lot of missionaries did. Because we were Mennonites and the Mennonite mission board was sending us out to do work on their behalf, they paid for everything.

But our big family cost the mission board a lot of money. Mama said once another missionary lady sidled up and asked if she knew about birth control. Mama was indignant and said of course she did, that she and Papa wanted a big family. They loved everyone of their four boys and four girls, and Ethiopia was a great place for children to grow up—except for the boarding school part.

Now we had a chance to talk to Paul. Would he tell us we should go into missions, maybe back to Ethiopia? Richard was surprised by what Paul said, but it was a timely word. Paul told him he thought he should go back to school, that the church needs educated people who understand the world and the mission of God in changing times and places.

Richard had secretly wanted to go back to school. He loved learning. In college he'd had a triple major, but he felt like there was so much work to be done, so many needs around the world, that we should jump right in. Now Paul was giving him permission to go study. He could study with a mission.

So we turned down all the calls to go into church and mission work and started applying for grad schools. With a second child on the way, this wouldn't be easy, but we were excited and believed that God would provide. We moved to Plain City, Ohio, to live with the

Showalter family for the summer. Part of that time David and Rhoda were in Kenya visiting Richard's younger brother Nate.

Richard learned Hebrew so he could get into the MDiv program at Associated Mennonite Biblical Seminary in Elkhart, Indiana, and from there into a doctoral program at Fuller Theological Seminary in Pasadena, California.

I loved the way Shiloh Mennonite Church welcomed us. There were so many babies and children. If Chad fussed in church, the women pulled out toys and snacks to share. Young girls came and carried him off to play. At EMC fussy babies just needed to be shushed up and hidden away so they didn't interrupt the concert or the lecture.

We picked strawberries and blackberries for freezing, canned pickles, beans, and tomatoes. We butchered chickens. The women of the church had a baby shower for Rhoda Jane born August 9, 1973. When she was a couple weeks old, we moved to Indiana to start the school year at AMBS.

The church networks in Ohio and Indiana helped us find housing. One family let us live in their basement apartment for a month. Another home was available for us to housesit without any rent for eight months while that family was in Florida. For the summer months we lived in yet another home—just to mow the grass and keep up the place. Three different homes for the year for just the price of utilities.

Other young moms in the church helped with childcare. It was hard staying home alone with two little children all day when Richard drove to seminary in our only car. We were way out in the country with no close neighbors. Sometimes Richard would go away for the weekend too, speaking in churches. The first time he was away overnight, and I was home alone with the two little children, I was so scared I could hardly sleep.

What if I accidentally cut myself with a knife when I was cooking, fainted and bled to death? The children were too little to phone someone or run for help. And at night when I lay down I was sure I heard a strange man rustling around under the bed. I froze, but nothing happened. I knew it was irrational. Finally, I slept, and the next morning read in Psalms 4, *"I will lie down in peace and sleep, for you alone, oh Lord, make me dwell in safety."*

You alone, oh Lord. Not my husband. Not a watchdog or a gun. You alone, oh Lord. I wanted this deep truth to become more real in my life. I copied the verse on index cards and posted one on the bathroom mirror, another on the bedroom mirror over the dresser, and one on the kitchen cupboard right over the sink.

Some friends of ours, Mel and Edna Shetler and their young family, were working with troubled youth in Goshen. Teen Haven, they called it. We jumped in to help—along with other young people. Richard and Mel worked together to charter a church out of the youth ministry so the kids could have a community, a "Body" to belong to. Later it got called Maple City Chapel and grew into one of the largest churches in Goshen.

I didn't realize it at the time, but it seems that we were good at starting things. Not always staying around to oversee what happened but kicking things off. That's what happened at Teen Haven. We loved the deep friendships we had and the way it felt like Acts 2 all over again. The early church sharing things in common, praying, and looking out for each other. I was starting to feel like maybe I belonged. I didn't like wearing a Mennonite covering, but if that's what it took to belong, these were my people.

One day I went for a walk on a back country road and an Amish buggy rolled by. I was praying about the need to wear Mennonite coverings and dresses all the time. It felt like an unwanted and unneeded burden. Like some relic from the past. The women in Plain City, Ohio, dressed like this and here at Teen Haven too. But they'd never lived in Ethiopia or Chicago. They'd lived in Goshen all their lives. Or maybe Lancaster or Rosedale.

Richard's parents really liked coverings and simple, modest Mennonite dresses. I liked their church and community even though I didn't like the distinctive attire. Once David, Richard's father, asked Richard if he didn't think my dresses were too short. Richard told me. He didn't want to hurt me and make me change who I was and what I was used to, but I never forgot what his father said. I was sure he wished his son had married someone else, someone more conservative who fit in better and didn't feel like they came in from the outside. Someone who gladly dressed in cape dresses and coverings all the time. Could I belong? Have one without the other? Probably not.

As I walked, I remembered Jesus in the Garden of Gethsemane, the night before he died—wrestling with thoughts of that cross. He asked God if it was possible to take "the cup" away, but in the end said he'd trust God and that it wasn't his will that mattered, but God's. He knew that for the good of the world, he'd have to go to the cross.

Now I knew my suffering was nothing like that of Jesus. But that day as the buggy clopped by, I felt like my Mennonite covering was a cross. "Not my will, but thine be done." Jesus said that. If he could go to the cross, then for God's sake, I could wear a covering! It was for the good of my family, the community—and maybe, even the world.

One day I took the children to a women's sewing circle at Mount Joy Mennonite Church, one of the churches in our network. I couldn't get much done, but there were other young moms and children playing together while we quilted and knotted comforters. Everyone was talking about an accident the day before. It had snowed and young guys were racing their snowmobiles across the frozen fields. One old conservative Mennonite lady with a big basket covering with black strings told the story.

It was dark and John was racing his snowmobile. It was a strange field, and he didn't know there was a thin electric fence around the edge. Just one wire stretched taut between fence posts. John ran right into the wire—and it cut off his head—just like that. His head rolled off onto the snow with blood spurting out.

The old lady shook her head sadly. Too bad it happened to someone only 18 years old, but it was the will of God. And we shouldn't grieve too much. "Everything happens for a reason."

What? The will of God? Surely God didn't want things like that to happen to anyone. He loved us and was weeping with John's family right now—like Jesus as Lazarus' tomb. Of course, John shouldn't have been riding in a strange field and going so fast, but to blame it on God? This wasn't the same God I was learning to trust with my safety at night, the God who'd provided a home for us to live rent-free while Richard was in grad school, the God who laid down his life for us.

14

Off to California

Rhoda was barely one, and Chad three, when we set out for southern California to study at Fuller Theological Seminary. Richard and two men from Teen Haven drove Mel Shetler's pickup out to California with a load of our things in the back. They drove straight through, taking turns driving and sleeping.

Later we brought the rest of the things in our car and camped along the way. Five long days from Goshen to Pasadena. We'd drive all day until nearly dark, then camp, and in the morning pack up and set out again. We drove an old Plymouth that Richard got for only $185. It didn't have AC, but low mileage, and ran pretty good even though it was old.

In California we stayed the first couple days with Irene Zook, an old schoolteacher friend of Mother Showalter's from Delaware. Then we met Donald and Barbara King, the pastor couple at Faith Mennonite Church in Downy on the southside of Los Angeles. We'd agreed to lead a Voluntary Service Unit for the Mennonite Board of Missions. This was something the church had wanted for a long time—young people to help lead boys' and girls' clubs, to help with leading the youth group, and support the work of the little mission church.

Richard would study in the seminary but we'd do whatever we could to help the church. The mission board rented a small home for our family and a nearby apartment for three Voluntary Service girls who made up our unit. I'd cook supper for the unit each night, and we'd have weekly Bible studies and recreation nights together as a unit.

We didn't know how we were going to make it without much income, but because we were helping the church, the mission board paid for our basic living expenses. They even paid gas mileage for things we did with the church and medical insurance, except maternity.

God had called us back to school. That was part of our mission for this season, and as long as he provided the funds, Richard would study.

We loved the little Mennonite church. We felt at home even though people didn't farm and wear coverings. The core members had moved from the Dakotas during the dustbowl days and taken up lawn-care work, the closest thing to urban farming. They felt a little out of place in the big city and didn't want to lose their children. They liked that we did things with the youth. One of the men told us, "The devil's got my kids."

Sometimes people who didn't have Mennonite background came too. Like a man who just got out of prison. He was part of our small group. And another couple where the man was a Mennonite who did VS in the city but married a woman who wasn't even a Christian. But she said she wanted to be a Christian and her favorite song was "Jesus Loves Me." She'd never heard it before.

There were maybe 30 to 40 of us, and we kept inviting young people from our street. One day a woman came to our home and said she'd never told anyone else, but before she was married, she'd gotten pregnant and had an abortion. This was back in 1972 before abortion was legal, and she felt terribly guilty, especially now that she saw how wild her own teenagers were. She wanted to get right with God. We all cried and prayed together. Soon one of her co-workers began coming to church and wanted to be a Christian too. Sometimes Richard preached and usually led the adult Sunday school class. We organized small groups that met in homes.

One day when little Rhoda was being noisy and naughty in church, Richard took her out and spanked her. They came back and she sat sniffling on his lap, nice and quiet the rest of the service. That's how Mennonites handled their children back in Ohio.

But a lady came up to Richard after church and asked him to please not spank his child again. She said if Rhoda was restless and naughty, she'd look after her in the basement.

Things were confusing at the seminary too. Richard had thought he wanted to get a ThD in historical theology, but the longer he spent time in the stacks studying the concept of "life" in the works of the Apostle Paul, the deader he felt. And we were running out of money for tuition.

One day as Richard wrestled with his feelings he felt God asking him if he was willing to give up his doctoral studies. This seemed bizarre. Hadn't God called him back to school to study with a mission? And we'd moved all the way across the country. But it almost felt like God asking Abraham if he was willing to sacrifice his son Isaac.

I was not happy. I'd sacrificed a lot to make this move and was supportive of his studies, and now just drop out?

Richard was at the seminary, wrestling with God. He went into a small chapel and as he knelt on the floor at the front crying out to God for clarity, the sunlight shone through the chapel window frame creating the shadow of a cross that fell on the pages of his Bible. He knew he had to drop out even if it didn't make sense and his own wife didn't think he should.

Although he'd cultivated his walk with God and remained committed to the Kingdom of Christ Richard recognized that he was more and more enamored with and captured by an intellectualism which gave little room for the humility of Christ.

We'd also run out of money for tuition. Richard decided to register as a special student in the School of World Missions instead of the School of Theology. Later he could drop the classes and just work for the church if tuition money didn't come through.

When he got back from registering for classes, there was a letter in the mail from our friends at Teen Haven in Goshen, Indiana. They'd taken up an offering for us and there was just enough tuition money for that semester.

The classes in the School of World Missions were so eye-opening Richard came back everyday bursting with excitement and saying these were the most interesting and relevant classes he'd ever taken—"the most exciting months of my entire formal education." It revolutionized his understandings of the world and his own Mennonite culture.

Jewel with daughter Rhoda Jane.

It started to put his whole life in context. He understood why the little mountain church his family started in Kentucky never took root locally—why they'd always been outsiders, why the locals didn't take to plain suits, cape dresses, and coverings even though non-conformity was preached with conviction.

As he studied courses in cultural anthropology, history of missions, and church growth we began to understand why God had called us to Fuller. We'd always wanted to be involved in the work of the church, and we began to understand in new ways how churches grow and how people movements happen in diverse cultures around the world.

An awareness of the many tribes and nations around the world where the gospel had never been preached, gripped our hearts. We weren't being called to study the concept of "life" in the works of the Apostle Paul, we were being called to live the life of Paul in the "regions beyond."

Richard's parents, with Grandma Amelia Swartzentruber who now lived with them, and their three younger children, took this opportunity to travel west. My sister Sara and her husband Gerald also began studies at Fuller as did Richard's younger brother Nate who was just returning from a term of service in Kenya. It was nice to have family around. California had felt like a foreign country.

We took the Showalter family to the Pacific for a swim and a beach picnic. Chad and Rhoda enjoyed the attention of their cool young Uncles Jon and Joe and their Aunt Audrey. We chose our picnic site and scattered out to enjoy the beach. When it was time to eat, we clustered around the table, but Chad was nowhere to be found.

Richard had last seen him playing in the rocks at the edge of the water. He ran there. Others fanned out up and down along the beach. I waited at our picnic table backed against a high cliff in a long row of other picnic spots.

As he ran north along the beach Richard spotted—way in the distance—a woman walking up the beach with a small, crying child. As he closed the distance, he saw it was his sister Audrey carrying a small boy. It was Chad! Audrey had found him with a kind woman who was walking slowly up the beach trying to help the lost child find his parents.

Apparently, he'd come to the picnic area and when he mistakenly came to the wrong table, took off running down the beach looking for us.

This experience led to one of Richard's most memorable sermons. The following year when he preached at a large mission meeting in Lancaster, Pennsylvania, he hoisted Chad on to his shoulders and preached from Luke 15 on the parable of the lost sheep.

"Nothing was more important than finding my lost son," he said, inviting the audience to enter into the great love of the Father for his lost and straying children. While he preached, Chad rested his chin on his father's head and smiled contentedly. The lost had been found.

At the beginning of our second school year in California, Richard came back from a doctor's appointment to check on an unusual swelling we'd noticed in one of his testicles. The doctor suspected cancer and wanted him to schedule surgery immediately.

Matthew had been born September 1975. We were busy young parents, running a VS unit, full-time graduate studies for Richard, and heavy involvement in the little church.

Matthew's birth completed our family of three children.

Matthew's birth had been a frightening yet rewarding experience. Richard had not been present for the other two births. Chad had been born in Virginia on March 24, 1971. A silver-haired gentlemanly doctor scheduled me to be induced when I showed up for an appointment dilated to 3 cm. He sent Richard home saying they'd call when the baby was born—no need to worry and pace in the waiting room.

A saddle block when the baby crowned and then forceps with a mirror adjusted for mom to see what was happening was the progressive way to give birth in 1971 Virginia. I didn't like the doctor's patronizing, just-trust-me, don't-worry-your-pretty-little-head attitude. Besides I got splitting headaches from the saddle block.

Rhoda was born in Ohio. We went to classes for moms and dads. Mount Carmel Hospital allowed dads in the delivery room if they went through the classes and wore scrubs. Richard was all in but was still down admitting me when Rhoda was born shortly after we arrived at the hospital. Her birth was totally natural and almost unattended—caught by a nurse and medical intern on duty on the night of August 9, 1973.

So this time Richard said he was not leaving my side. Besides, being in VS, we didn't have maternity insurance. We engaged the services of a hippie doctor who specialized in home births. He'd told us to call his pager when contractions were about 15 minutes apart, but before he could leave the movie theater and drive across Los Angeles, Richard had delivered Matthew Daniel in our double bed on September 10, 1975.

Now, just five months since Matthew's unusual birth, I waited at the hospital while my husband underwent surgery. I left tiny Matthew with a friend in the car to go meet the surgeon. He came toward me in the hall, pulling off his mask. I thought they'd have to do a biopsy to know for sure it was cancer. I still held out hope, but the surgeon said matter-of-factly, "It's cancer."

"How can you know without a biopsy?" I challenged.

He sighed and looked into my naïve, hopeful eyes. "Because I've seen it often enough. We just don't know what kind. Some kinds spread rapidly, and Richard's cancer looks like the spreading kind. He'll need a second surgery to remove all the lymph nodes from his abdominal cavity. And radiation. Go home and help Richard recover. We'll get the biopsy report then discuss the details."

I ran out into the bright California noon, angry that the sun was shining. It should have hidden its face from such dark news, and there it was looking all bright and cheerful as if to say, "all's right with the world!" I wanted to scream. Instead, I sat in the car and nursed Matthew, watching his tiny fingers fondle the buttons on my blouse. Peaceful, content, and totally oblivious to the fact that he'd most likely be growing up without a father.

Richard came home the next day. He quickly recovered from the first surgery and life resumed its almost normal rhythm. One afternoon as the children napped and I was alone in the living room I knelt beside the threadbare black and brown tweed couch.

I was angry, not only at the sun, but at the Creator of the sun. Why was he allowing this to happen? We were such good people, a nice little family. We had given him our lives. We wanted to serve him, maybe even be missionaries. We'd moved away from our families, all the way across the country to continue preparing for service. And now this? Didn't God need us?

"Why, God, why?" I whisper-screamed, pounding the couch cushions as dust mites swirled up in the slanting sunlight.

"Jewel, you have to trust me." I heard a deep, quiet voice in my spirit.

"Trust you?" I thought I had been trusting God ever since I was a little girl sitting on my father's lap, knowing that God was a Father who never left me even when I went away to boarding school. I'd learned not to be afraid at night alone with the children. I'd even agreed to wear a covering for the peace of the family and community.

Now this voice angered me deeply. I heard it again. "Jewel, you have to trust me."

I felt like I'd invested all my money in the God-bank. That bank had gone under, and now the bank president was calling and asking me to invest more money. "Not in your bank!" I retorted. "You let me down!"

The voice came a third time. "Jewel, you have to trust me."

What if I don't? My racing mind scrambled, searching for options. If I didn't trust him, what other options were there? God or a never-ending, empty, black nothingness. No Creator and sustainer. No purpose in life. Nothing to live for.

I started weeping, and I chose. "God, I trust you. No matter what happens. You are Lord. You know I want my husband to live. But I give him to you. Whether he lives or dies, I trust you to fulfil your purposes."

I worked around the VS unit with a new sense of rest and peace. While washing the breakfast dishes one morning a scripture reference popped into my mind. Luke 9:60. Luke 9:60. I had no idea what that verse was. I stopped to look it up. *Jesus said to him, "Let the dead bury their own dead, but you go and proclaim the kingdom of God."*

I panicked. Did this strange verse mean that Richard was going to die? As I waited before the Lord, I sensed the Spirit saying, "You've been paralyzed and obsessed with thoughts of death and dying. Leave those decisions to me. Your times are in my hand. Your husband is in my hand. Seek first the Kingdom!"

That weekend we attended a healing convention led by Agnes Sanford at Melodyland, a large charismatic church and Bible school nearby. After preaching, Sanford invited congregants to get in circles and pray for healing in each other's lives. As Richard moved to pray for others, I sensed the Lord asking me to pray for Richard's healing.

I'd not been able to do that, believing that if I prayed and he wasn't healed, I'd lose my faith. If I was going to lose my husband, I didn't want to lose my faith. I moved behind him and quietly prayed for healing.

The next week we met with the surgeon. He had good news. It wasn't the kind of cancer they'd first suspected. He wouldn't need further surgery, only two weeks of radiation treatment. Then if he was cancer free for five years, his chances of getting cancer were no greater than anyone else's.

15

A Home in Rosedale

After two years in California we were ready to travel east to Ohio. Rosedale Bible College was inviting Richard to teach. This would give us a chance to reconnect with family and church roots. And also make sure Richard's health was stable.

We traded our old gray Plymouth in on a half-ton pickup truck, loaded our things, crammed the five of us into the cab and headed east driving through the Arizona desert at night. One tearful young woman from the church had asked if she could pay for the children and me to fly while Richard drove the truck east by himself. Someone else took a look at our truck and said we reminded them of *The Grapes of Wrath*.

We took a southern route through Arizona and Arkansas, averaging 35 to 40 miles per hour. The worst part of the trip was a flat tire caused by a broken wheel rim. Too much weight on a little truck, the junk yard man said as he helped Richard find a new wheel and tire while the children and I waited in the scattered shade of a thorny shrub.

In Rosedale we rented an old farmhouse half a mile from the college nearby Shiloh Mennonite Church where Richard's father pastored. In California I'd taken to wearing a hippie kerchief instead of a white Mennonite covering, but that was edgy for the wife of the pastor's son.

Were these my people? They hadn't been to California. They didn't even like Chinese food. One night for fun we took the youth leaders out to a Chinese restaurant and all the man could talk about was how much he liked poor man's steak (a dish of hamburger patties in cream of mushroom soup) and mashed potatoes better than all the slimy things he couldn't pronounce.

Sometimes I resented needing to put on a Mennonite covering, but it was fun learning how to make applesauce, homemade bread, and cut sweet corn off the cobs for freezing.

I met other people who felt like they didn't fit in either. Everyone gets lonely, keeps looking for a place to belong. We started a home group with another family of newcomers. Someone who'd worked in Central America came. Young adults joined.

We were hungry to know God and follow him. We wanted to learn to know our neighbors who didn't go to Shiloh. We had a nice church, but what about people on the outside? Didn't Jesus say we should go from "Jerusalem to the ends of the earth?" If it was hard for me to wear a covering, what about the people in the "ends of the earth?" But if coverings were really what God wanted us to wear and it wasn't just a funny Mennonite thing, shouldn't we be willing to wear them?

The young women at Shiloh asked me to teach their Sunday School class. We were studying through the gospel of Luke and stopped short at Luke 14, *"when you give a feast, invite the poor, the crippled, the lame, the blind...don't invite those who can pay you back..."*

I asked the girls, "Do any of you know any poor people, anyone on welfare?" No one did.

Richard was teaching RBC classes like The Deeper Life, Strategy of Missions, Personal Evangelism. He began taking students with him to visit in the neighboring village of Mechanicsburg. Evangelism is best learned and practiced in real-life friendships and interactions.

One of the first homes they visited was a welfare mom living common-law with a man so she could continue to receive her benefits. The couple opened their home for a Bible study.

Linden and Charlene Good, students at RBC, moved to Mechanicsburg and found jobs. They opened their home for Bible studies. Rather than plugging into one of the local churches they said that our home group was their church.

Before we knew it and without much pre-planning, several Bible studies in Rosedale, Mechanicsburg, and London came together in Mechanicsburg for Sunday worship in the Goods' home. We soon outgrew that and banded together to buy a large home that came up for sale at 127 N. Main Street.

We removed several walls to create a large gathering place. The Mechanicsburg Christian Fellowship now had its own meeting space.

During this time, Richard and I were also exploring mission and service opportunities overseas. We wanted to focus on the least-reached regions of the world. Eastern Mennonite Missions talked with us about joining their team in Hong Kong. We started to think maybe God was leading us there. I'd always thought I might be called to China as a missionary, but after the communist revolution in 1948, that door swung shut. Now maybe it was beginning to open? Was this God's call? We took steps to plan in that direction. Richard told RBC he would not teach in the coming year.

The Mennonite community in Ohio was close, caring, and sweet. When we moved to Rosedale, a group of women helped me wash the dirty windows in our old farmhouse. Others helped wallpaper and paint. But it seemed like we weren't too good at including outsiders. People who weren't "born" Mennonite, who didn't have names like Miller, Yoder, Troyer, Gingerich, or Beachy. I was from Pennsylvania, but I'd married a Showalter, the pastor's son. The early Jewish church had trouble including Gentiles too, but they worked at it.

Mennonites kind of reminded me of Jews. Instead of circumcision we had coverings. Instead of kosher food we had homemade bread and pies, chicken and noodles and ham loaf. We couldn't trace our lineage all the way back to Abraham, but back to 1525 in Europe when those first believers' baptisms took place. We weren't at odds with the Roman empire but the European state churches had banned and burned us.

When we started coming to America in the 1600's, the government mostly ignored us. We were good, quiet farmers and honest tradesmen, but didn't fight in their Revolutionary and Civil wars. That caused a few problems for some people, especially southerners in the Civil War. Finally during WW II, the U.S. government came up with "alternative service" also known as Civilian Public Service (CPS) and later the 1-W program, for us conscientious objectors.

All that to say, it seemed like a big jump for someone who didn't have that Amish or Mennonite background to actually join our churches. But my whole childhood in Ethiopia was about including "outsiders." And today the Ethiopian Mennonite Church (Meserete Kristos) is the largest Mennonite church in the world.

Richard had grown up in southeastern Kentucky and their little church on Gays Creek was full of people with names like Stidham or Gay, although none of them became leaders. We wanted to be people who went from the "Jewish" Mennonites to the "Gentile" North Americans, Chinese or Turks. How might God use us in the "regions beyond" where the church was weak or non-existent?

As MCF quickly grew to 70-80 attenders, packing out the remodeled home, our family also grew. One of the early attenders was a woman with three young children, fleeing an abusive alcoholic husband. We took her into our home.

I woke up the next morning with the oldest boy rummaging through the kitchen cupboards looking for food. When I served breakfast, he dumped a whole box of cheerios into his bowl. The children had been food-deprived and ate everything in sight.

Should we encourage the woman to be reconciled with her abusive husband? Was divorce an option? And what about people who came to our doors who were already divorced and remarried? These were live issues in the "Gentile" church. A visiting speaker said MCF reminded him of the Corinthian church.

When the broader Conservative Mennonite Conference (now known as the Rosedale Network of Churches) learned that we were welcoming divorced and remarried people into the church, there was pushback. These were not issues most Mennonite churches had dealt with. Divorce was almost unknown among us.

Richard had been scheduled to hold renewal meetings in one of our network churches, but when they learned that we were welcoming "Gentiles" who were divorced and remarried into our fellowship, they disinvited him.

This slight stung. Traditional Mennonite friends were offended and scandalized by what they heard was happening at MCF. While we were thrilled to see new believers coming to faith, we also wanted to remain in close fellowship with our Mennonite network, our tribe, our people. We wanted to be respectful, to wrestle for God's way forward—like the "Jerusalem Council" in the book of Acts.

When Jesus walked on earth and admonished his followers not to offend "one of these little ones" wasn't he talking about new believers, "little children" who were young in the faith rather than the staunch, conservative pillars of the faith? Stuck in their ways, I might add, in my cynical moments. Were they stifling a new move of God, or truly "protecting the flock" under their care?

Meanwhile EMM accepted us for service in Hong Kong and brought us in for orientation. Richard had some health struggles which we wondered might be related to his earlier bout with cancer. He was weak and exhausted, not even able to mow the lawn. Eventually he grew stronger and was given a clean bill of health.

I took this as a sign that God was calling us to Hong Kong, but Richard did not feel at peace.

This unexpected change of plans clouded our relationship. I struggled to forgive Richard for the way he'd handled the decision. He acknowledged his failure of leadership and asked my forgiveness. How had we come to such an impasse? We'd always valued open sharing, submitting our thoughts and feelings to one another as we wrestled to come to consensual decisions.

Richard said he'd had doubts but hoped they'd change. It felt a bit like his decision to drop out of his ThD studies at Fuller. Not logical, but something God was asking us to do in obedience to him. We'd been poised to leave for Hong Kong, but lacking a mutual sense of peace and clarity, hunkered down in Mechanicsburg.

We clung to each other in confusion remembering our vows "for better, for worse..." Frozen in bewilderment I struggled to forgive.

One day as I prayed about the situation, I saw, very unexpectedly, a scene from high school English class, Miss Havisham, the jilted bride from Charles Dicken's *Great Expectations*. Decades after her hoped-for wedding day, the embittered old woman refused to change out of her yellowing wedding gown. She dedicated her life to chasing mice and roaches away from the moldering wedding cake.

As I pondered the unusual image, the Holy Spirit said, "That's you!" God showed me the ugliness of my unforgiveness. I was able to leave my regret, confusion, and unforgiveness behind and step forward into whatever God was calling us to—together.

Even as we walked with young believers and opened our lives and our home to anyone, we continued to wonder when God might release us to go to the "least reached" regions of the world. True, there were many needs here, but our little village was also filled with churches—Methodist, Baptist, Church of Christ, Pentecostal...

I wondered if I'd just gotten tired of trying to fit in, to belong. On one level I loved our Mennonite community and felt a bone-deep loyalty. I never considered going to another denomination. We had our weaknesses, but everyone does. Let's work to water our own grass, not just look for "greener pastures." But maybe it would be easier to do that on the other side of the globe than in the village next door?

How could we rightfully discern God's will? Together. Was our vision to serve overseas something God wanted us to give up? Was our desire to go overseas just a romantic notion, a failure to fit back into the close-knit Mennonite community?

In California I had taken to wearing little hippie kerchiefs on my head instead of the traditional white Mennonite covering. It helped me blend in more. But back here in Ohio, Shiloh Mennonite had a standard asking women to wear the traditional coverings. The box began to squeeze me. And maybe it wasn't even wise.

We discussed the changing culture around us and pondered cross-cultural ministry outside the Mennonite community. What felt good for us to wear in "Jerusalem" might not seem as appropriate in Judea, Samaria, and "the ends of the earth."

"These church standards make me feel bound," I told Richard. "I can't be myself. Who am I anyway?"

"Well, you won't feel bound if you're not fighting and resisting," he observed philosophically. "Living in community requires *gelassenheit,* yieldedness."

"Well then, what does *gelassenheit* mean for you?" I retorted.

One morning the wife of an MCF elder called. Haltingly she shared a word she sensed God wanted her to share. Habakkuk 2:3: *"The vision is for an appointed time...Though it tarries, wait for it."*

God used this special word to draw Richard and me even closer together. He made it clear that he wanted us to wholeheartedly plug into the work in Mechanicsburg, to submit to the leadership of the local Mennonite church. Perhaps, at a later time, we'd be released to serve overseas.

Since Richard had resigned from his RBC teaching we had no regular salary. The young church began to share tithes and offerings with us. Itinerant speaking, substitute teaching, and free-lance writing provided sporadic income, but the balance in the check book fell to $2. At the grocery store check-out, I returned unnecessary items from my cart back to the shelves. We could live without cream cheese.

Our home and church became a center for hurting and broken people. One morning a distraught woman stumbled in, disheveled and weeping. We embraced her and drew our children into a prayer circle around her. She'd been attending church. She and her young son occasionally overnighted with us. Later seven-year-old Rhoda asked, "Mommy, what's rape?"

We enjoyed our open home but struggled to love like Jesus. One woman dropped in to say she needed help to buy de-lousing shampoo for her four children. I was standing six feet across the room when I heard Jesus say, "Give her a hug!"

Another day I was short and snappy—without time for devotional prayer and Bible reading. Richard sensed that I was overwhelmed and needed quiet time to focus. He took our three children and several other neighborhood kids who all but lived with us out to hoe corn.

As I slumped down with Bible in hand, I wished my scheduled reading program for the day was not in the book of Revelation. I'd never enjoyed this colorful book with its symbolic hills, harlots and dragons. I needed something from the Gospels, like *"come unto me, all you who are weary and heavy laden...I will give you rest."*

I dutifully opened to my scheduled reading for the day, Rev. 19, then began to cry as I read v. 7, *"Hallelujah! For the Lord God Almighty reigns. Let us rejoice and be glad and give him glory. For the wedding of the Lamb has come, and his bride has made herself ready. Fine linen, bright and clean, was given her to wear." (Fine linen stands for the righteous acts of the saints.)*

At that moment I felt the indescribable joy of a bride on her wedding day and knew, that in Mechanicsburg, God was giving me the opportunity to create a wedding gown of exquisite beauty.

There was limited time and money. But we worked to use what we had. Instead of going out to eat we'd have "Mommy's McDonalds" with homemade burgers and fries. On Christmas eve we planned a family-only dinner with Richard's favorite oyster stew. For the first time since we were married, I got out my pink and gray wedding china. I put on a green linen tablecloth and set only five places.

We'd agreed on a family-only evening, but as darkness fell and I lit candles the phone rang. It was Richard. He'd gone to visit a young man from the youth group who'd landed in the juvenile detention center. We'd heard the juveniles would be allowed to go home on Christmas Eve. Richard told me this boy's family did not want him. He was all alone. Richard paused, then asked what I thought we should do. We opened our "inn" on Christmas eve.

Richard's frequent travel and church work left little time for the two of us to talk. Misunderstandings and disappointments mounted even though we were committed to new levels of transparency and consensual decision-making. We were learning each other's strengths and weaknesses.

As little irritations mounted, I began a list of the problems, things HE needed to improve on the home front. I kept the list in my pocket Bible, using it as a marker, waiting the opportune time to bring things up. I didn't want to be a nag, but...

One day I heard loud screams as Matthew came home from kindergarten yelling, "It won't come out! It won't come out!" He ran into the kitchen, pulling on his nose.

As Matt and his friend walked the two blocks home from school, they tromped through little piles of field corn that had spilled from the harvest wagons wending their way to the grain elevator, the tallest structure in our little country town of 2,000. The boys began to stick kernels of corn up their noses and snorted them out to see whose kernel would go the furthest. Only one time Matt's kernel didn't come out. By the time he reached home the now-swollen kernel was well-lodged near the bridge of his nose.

I grabbed a nut pick from the utensil drawer and tried to extract the kernel as he continued to sob, wondering if he'd die. I turned him upside down, held the other nostril shut, and commanded him to blow hard. It didn't work. I was determined not to take him to the doctor. Funds were limited, and we didn't have insurance.

Would the vacuum cleaner work? I hauled it from the closet. But it was old with suction so weak I wasn't always sure the house was any cleaner after we'd finished cleaning. The watching children couldn't help saying, "Oh, gross!" as they watched my frantic endeavors to extract the kernel and calm my now-hysterical son.

Finally, I knew we'd have to go to the doctor. I shouldered my purse and took Matthew to the downtown doctor's office. They'd see us, but there was a wait for walk-ins. I settled Matt with some toys and sat down to read. I looked for a distracting book in my purse but found only my pocket Bible. I jerked it out angrily, and it fell open to the spot I'd marked with the list of my husband's faults.

I began reading. *"Love is patient, love is kind. It does not envy, it does not boast, it is not proud. It is not rude, it is not self-seeking, it is not easily angered, **it keeps no record of wrongs...**"* (I Corinthians 13:4-5).

"Love keeps no record of wrongs..." that convicting verse fragment whose place had been marked out by the list of my husband's short-comings. I wept with conviction, crumpled up that petty list, and threw it in the wastebasket just as the nurse called us in.

With one flick of the doctor's shiny silver probe, the offending kernel popped out onto the floor—the most expensive kernel of corn in the world, but one that taught me a priceless lesson. To this day I can't remember a single thing on that list.

During these days of church planting in Mechanicsburg, I was also spending time with a group of Yokefellow volunteers who led weekly Bible studies and fellowship times for 20-30 women at the Ohio Reformatory for Women in nearby Marysville.

One evening I shared a prayer concern with a circle of prisoners, asking their advice. A new believer at MCF had left her alcoholic husband. We were also reaching out to the husband, praying for his salvation. Should the wife return to him? Would her love and respect ultimately win him to Christ? Or was she free to leave? I was loathe to give any grounds for unfaithfulness and divorce.

One prisoner, a wiry, little woman with mousy brown hair fixed her intense blue eyes on me. "Don't make that woman go back with that man," she said. "I tried to stay with a drunk man. My church made me go back and look where it got me."

"What happened?" I was afraid to ask. "I shot him," she said.

Case closed.

Richard and I had reached out to begin MCF before he was ordained. He'd been leading, teaching, and preaching since he was a teenager. He loved people and absorbed history, information, and ideas like a dry sponge. One Sunday morning he was down on all fours horsing around with Chad and Rhoda as I popped a casserole in the oven for lunch. I knew he was scheduled to teach the adult Sunday school class that morning and chided, "Have you prepared for your class?" I hadn't seen him crack his Sunday School quarterly.

He gave me a sideways grin and said, "I've been preparing all my life."

It was not unusual to see him sit on the front bench and prayerfully scribble notes for an upcoming sermon on the back of an envelope or piece of scrap paper in his Bible. I loved his simple, scholarly-in-a-non-academic-way sermons that moved people to repentance and transformation.

When MCF mushroomed he was the logical person to become pastor, but that would have been presumptuous. He was not yet ordained. Even as we explored the possibility of other ordained men giving leadership the congregation requested his ordination.

Part of the communal discernment in the calling of pastors in our community entailed asking the members of our church, Shiloh Mennonite, whether there were objections or affirmation for such a call. And in the weeks leading up to ordination, conference leaders interviewed the pastoral couple and shared any questions or objections that may have surfaced from the community.

As Richard and I went through this communal discernment the conference oversight team said there was widespread affirmation for Richard's ordination but noted that someone had shared a concern about our children being too unruly.

That hurt. In California people thought we shouldn't spank our children, and here in Ohio people thought we should—more!

I fell on my bed, once again weeping in confusion. "God, I want to please you, not be tossed about by everyone's opinions. But these are my people. I want to fit in here. But most of all I want to hear your affirming and refining words."

Suddenly the phone rang. I quickly dried my tears and reached for the receiver on the nightstand. Someone in Pennsylvania wanted me to come in to speak at a conference on "Creative Child Rearing." They even wanted me to write a regular column for the *Festival Quarterly* called "Family Creations."

Then in a Yokefellow Bible study at the Ohio Reformatory of Women, the speaker of the evening taught on how childhood experiences and memories affect adult behavior. He prayed for the healing of painful memories that—unbeknownst to us—may still be affecting our behavior.

Suddenly Mrs. Wallace's face surfaced in my mind. Why now? I wondered. That's in the past. I've forgotten and forgiven her. But have I really?

The Holy Spirit probed, "Haven't you been afraid to discipline your children, not wanting to punish them unjustly even when they justly deserve to be set straight?"

After that unjust spanking from Mrs. Wallace when I'd been forced to lie, I had vowed that I'd never do that to my children. I asked God to heal that painful memory and free me to relate to my children in life-giving ways.

***

Many Sunday mornings a big, pleasant man who daily roamed the village while living on his SSI funds for mental health issues, would stand in the back of the church during the worship time. He especially loved the popular new worship song, "Our God Reigns" and began calling us the "Our God Reigns Church." I loved that we could be a church for all people.

When we pondered what it meant to be a church for all Richard often repeated the phrase, "We will not reject anyone our Lord has received." Everyone is to be welcomed and discipled to follow Jesus. Someone else said, "I hope we always have smokers at our church––but not the same ones!"

An unchurched family with four children began attending. Their two teenage sons joined the youth group, and we were pleased with their commitment and spiritual growth. They all signed up to come to the church campout.

As some of us gathered to begin swimming and cooking supper, the two teenage boys dashed into the lake and swam out to a raft in the middle. As they turned to swim back, one of the boys cried for help and sank. We stood helplessly on the shore. There was no lifeguard. Richard knew I could swim and ran up asking that I go to the rescue. The young man had gone down for a second time and not resurfaced.

I hesitated for precious seconds, still dressed in shoes and a heavy jean skirt. I didn't want to strip to my underwear.

"Go!" Richard urged. I pulled off my skirt and dove in. I found his body under the dark green water and began towing it to shore. Someone called EMS. Others formed a human chain out into the deep and helped pull in his body. We began CPR on the beach. The squad arrived. They found a pulse and sped away.

He was on a respirator for several days. We were hopeful. But his brain swelled from the lack of oxygen, and our young church held its first funeral. My hesitation and concern for appearances had proved fatal.

16

Off to Kenya and Turkey

Richard, Matthew, and Rhoda squeezed into two airplane seats to give a distraug
mother and her baby space on a crowded airplane.

We began hearing that Rosedale Mennonite Missions was putting together a team to pioneer mission work in Turkey. They had overseas work in Costa Rica, Nicaragua, and Ecuador, but sensed it was time to open a new field among the least-reached peoples in what was being called "the 10/40 window." The centers of Islam, Hinduism, and Buddhism all lay between these two parallels.

175

Missionaries were not welcome unless they came as professionals teaching English or beginning businesses.

The mission board president, David I. Miller, invited us to lead the Turkey initiative. Another young couple, Merle and Mary Hochstedler, had already accepted RMM's invitation to serve on this pioneer team and were taking a year of study at the Fuller School of World Mission.

Both Richard and I were deeply stirred by this call from our conference mission board. It felt right. We had planted a growing church in "our own back yard." And Richard liked to say that overseas missions was just doing what you've already been doing in another "back yard."

It was hard to think of leaving the young church in Mechanicsburg, but Linden and Charlene Good had a heart for the village and sensed that God was calling them to give their lives there. The church blessed us––glad to help send and support us for the "regions beyond."

In a deeply moving commissioning service one woman sang an original song over us from John 15, *"You have not chosen me, but I have chosen you and ordained you that you should go and bring forth fruit, and that your fruit should remain. That whatsoever you shall ask the Father in my* name, *He may give it you."*

We sold our home on Walnut Street, behind the church, and packed for overseas. While Turkey was our long-term destination, we planned to spend most of a year in Kenya on the way. We'd learned of a revival among young adults in Kenya. They called themselves names like "Guerillas for Christ" or "Regions Beyond Ministry" and its "School of Ministry." They gave themselves to street preaching and youth camps. Many had grown up in nominally Christian churches but were really getting "born again" and filled with the Holy Spirit.

Several of these fiery young men and women found their way to Rosedale Bible College, forging a partnership that blessed the little Mennonite school as well as helped to equip a generation of leaders for ministry in Kenya.

Although we planned to move to the Turkish world where there were scarcely any Christians from Muslim background, we wanted to experience the church in a place where it was growing rapidly.

The night before we left, we slept at David and Rhoda Showalter's home in Plain City, Ohio. Richard and I slept in a double bed in their guest room with the children sprawled in sleeping bags on the floor of the room. Our ten big suitcases filled the living room downstairs.

On the morning of our departure, I woke before anyone else, filled with doubt and foreboding. The evening before we'd had a farewell with close friends and family members. I saw our children's pain as they cried and clung to their friends and relatives.

Was it right to make our children suffer like this? Would they hate us—and the God we served—for dragging them away from all that was cozy and familiar? What if we were making a terrible mistake taking them away from the community we'd come to love?

In the gray light of early dawn, I turned to the Bible on the nightstand. It fell open to Psalm 90. *"Lord, you have been our dwelling place throughout all generations. Before the mountains were born or you brought forth the earth and the world, from everlasting to everlasting you are God..."*

This was a prayer of Moses, a man who wandered in the wilderness for more than 40 years. A shepherd. A nomad. But he knew God as his "dwelling place." And that's what I wanted most for our children. It didn't matter the kind of house we had, or where that house was located.

"Oh God, help me, us, our children, to know what it means to dwell in you," I prayed. "It doesn't take a white picket fence, a yard, a weeping willow tree, Mennonite neighbors. You can use all those things––or none of them. Only let us dwell in you, find our home in you—now and forever."

Henry Mulandi met us in Kenya. He'd been a student at RBC and welcomed us to Thika, the home of RBM, a ministry he had founded. Simon Nderitu, a member of the RBM team, taught at Mangu High School and offered to let us live with him in his two-bedroom home on the high school compound. Richard and I shared a twin bed, and the children slept on floor mats.

Quickly we learned how to live without a refrigerator, oven, hot running water, car, or phone. We learned how to cook with local staples and use crowded buses and matatus. Sometimes we rode in cars owned by Kenyan friends as we went to high schools and churches for conferences and rallies. I was trying to homeschool the children, but the books we'd ordered hadn't arrived.

We learned to pray fervently—out loud, to dance, sway, and clap. Songs came in English, Swahili, Kikuyu, or other tribal languages. Richard enjoyed the energetic preaching and jumped right in to work with translators. They wanted us to teach them new praise and worship songs which quickly took on their own flair and cadence.

One evening as Richard preached I was trying to occupy the children in the back of the auditorium. They were restless and unhappy after yet another meal of bland cornmeal-mush *ugali* with cooked cabbage. Shortly after the conference, all three of them came down with hepatitis. But that evening Richard preached on the story of Mary—breaking her flask of costly ointment to anoint the feet of Jesus. He invited respondents to the front of the large auditorium, asking if we were willing to give Jesus that which was most valuable to us.

I was strangely moved by Richard's sermon. Often I had on my feedback hat, thinking of things to share with him, or I was entertaining the children with sketches or outlines. But that evening I heard the Spirit speak through my husband's sermon.

I don't have anything of value left, I mused. Only used clothing and a bare minimum of kitchen furnishings. No hidden stash of material things. The only things of value left in my life, my only "possessions"—were my children! I was sobered by how difficult this experience had become for them. Especially Chad who had made it very clear that he did not want to leave Ohio for the unknowns of Kenya and Turkey. In choosing to come, we needed to almost disregard his feelings.

As I knelt on the bare cement floor of the school auditorium, I sensed the Spirit's whisper, "When valuable things are broken, fragrance is released." And so I gave my children, once again, to Jesus. "They are yours!" I cried. "Use their lives to waft abroad the fragrance of the gospel!"

The breaking glass of Mary's perfume flask seemed violent and wasteful to the spectators, but Jesus said, "She has done a beautiful thing."

As we travelled from convention to convention, we never knew where we'd eat or sleep. One week in the town of Naivasha, our family of five was given a small room with three single beds for the week. As we readied for bed I explained to the children that Richard and I would share the one twin bed, Rhoda would have her own twin, and Chad and Matt would share the other twin.

Chad declared loudly that he would NOT sleep with his younger brother, but since there were no other options but the bare cement floor, I situated a boy at each end of the bed and drew an imaginary diagonal line between them.

In front of an African home.

Sometime in the wee hours of the night I heard an angry yell from Chad, "I'm all wet!"

Matthew, who had not wet his bed since he was potty trained, had thoroughly soaked himself and his older brother. I remembered my own wet boarding school beds. Bed wetting can be a sign of insecurity.

But the next morning Richard and the excited team of Kenyan young adults set off for another rally. "Oh Mama Chad (a Kenyan title of respect for a woman who has borne a child), God is really working! Pray for us," they said as they headed out the door singing and clapping. I was left with stinking sheets and three very unhappy children.

I drew cold water and filled a large, galvanized metal tub in the washroom. I socked the yellow sheets down into the cold water, then hung them outside to dry on a barbed wire fence. So what if God is moving among the Kenyan youth? I needed an automatic washer and some schoolbooks!

The next night came, and Chad declared more loudly than the night before that under no circumstances would he ever sleep with his brother again. His last night's objections were now grounded in objective evidence.

I told him—just as emphatically—that there were no other options and mollified him by praying really hard that Matthew wouldn't wet the bed again. We were, after all, adjusting a bit and feeling more secure by now.

But sadly, that night there was another midnight wail. This time Matthew not only wet the bed but also threw up all over his older brother.

The next morning the ministry team trooped off to the conference—where God continued to "really work," and I was left with more stinking sheets and restless children.

As I tried to wash the sheets again, I was overwhelmed by the way this experience with all its unpleasant uncertainties was unfolding. Richard, ever the pioneering explorer, excelled at "making do" and wanted his family to enjoy the unexpected adventures with him along the way.

Anger welled up inside as I rehearsed the frank conversation I was going to have about how this latest adventure was going. I felt little love for him or the Kenyan church. I wasn't willing to wash those sheets one more night! And we still had three nights to go.

As I knelt on the wet concrete and prepared—once again—to sock those stinking sheets down into the cold water of the floor tub I heard the voice of Jesus ask, "Jewel, are you willing to wash those sheets for me?"

"Oh God," I sobbed. I knew I wasn't willing to wash them for my husband, my children, or the Kenyan church. "When you put it that way... I'm doing all this for you? You noticed? And you want me to work at it with all my heart?" My hot tears took the chill off the water, and I broke before God in that damp gray washroom. He was pleased with my service. I could do it for him.

This experience transformed me, not our sleeping accommodation. Several weeks later we found ourselves in a remote Kenyan village. That night in a thatched hut with muddy puddles on the dirt floor, our whole family was given only one bed to sleep in. It was slightly wider than a twin bed, but not as wide as a double.

"Children, we all get to sleep together in one bed tonight," I enthused. Before we crawled in I drew a little diagram with Richard and me at one end and the three children at the other and where our legs should be. No one wet the bed that night.

***

Meanwhile the first part of our Turkey team had arrived, and we were expected to join three months later. We took time to visit Egypt, Israel, and the West Bank enroute to Turkey, spending an unforgettable Christmas Eve on Manger Square in Bethlehem, singing "Hark the Herald Angels Sing" in the Shepherds' Field. We took walking tours of Jerusalem while staying at an Arab youth hostel in Jerusalem.

Early one morning we caught a taxi to the Tel Aviv airport with all our luggage. We were excited and ready to catch our chartered tourist flight to Egypt and then a connecting flight to begin our new life in Istanbul. But there was a delay and then another delay.

Three plane loads of angry travelers milled around the crowded lounge. We weren't allowed to leave security. The airport officials issued lunch vouchers. Tempers flared. Babies cried and still no word about the long delay. A photographer for *Life Magazine* caught in the group spent his time snapping photos of irate travelers and agents, telling us that was one of his favorite photojournalism topics.

Ticket agents distributed dinner vouchers. Still no movement. By now it was dark. Then the agent came in and began distributing green, pink, and blue slips of paper to everyone. Our family got green. Then he made his announcement. Everyone who had received green and pink slips of paper would be allowed to board the only two planes that were available. All the people with blue slips would have to wait until tomorrow when another plane would be available. They'd be given vouchers for a hotel overnight.

All greens and pinks smiled with guilty relief to be the lucky ones to finally leave the terminal. We noticed that the young mother whose baby had cried much of the day had received a blue slip. Now she tearfully pled with the agent to see if she could be permitted to go. Her baby was sick and needed attention.

The ticket agent came on the PA system asking if any green or pink ticket holders would be willing to exchange their ticket with the young mother and her sick baby. Stony silence. Everyone looked down. No one volunteered. He asked again. Begged us to show compassion. No one budged.

Richard suggested we offer to give up our tickets to help the young mom. There were five of us. We wouldn't be separated, but we'd give up our tickets if that would help.

The travel agent conferred, checked his list, then came back with a suggestion. "I can tell you're a good Christian family," he said. "And you have little children. Would you mind sitting two of your children in one seat, and then we could just squeeze this young woman and her baby in?"

We didn't mind and arrived in Cairo just in time to catch our connecting flight to Istanbul.

We arrived in Istanbul knowing scarcely a word of Turkish. Our teammates met us with dictionaries, mini tape recorders, and loop tapes. We were quickly schooled in the Language Acquisition Made Practical (LAMP) method of "learn a little and use it a lot" with the services of a language helper to record phrases and then practice them multiple times along an established language route.

Memorizing the texts like parrots, then repeating them on the streets was brutal. First day: "Hi, my name is Jewel. I want to learn Turkish. This is all I can say." Second day: "Hi my name is Jewel. I'm from America. We're looking for a host family to live with."

We jumped in immediately, using bilingual hotel staff to record our first dialogs as we hunkered down in a hotel room in Kadikoy, on the Asian side of Istanbul, determined to find a host family with whom we could lodge and bond for the first few months.

Friendly business owners along the street looked forward to our coming, wondering what new things we could say that day. They became our teachers. One man said it was like a *foto roman*—the continued comics that ran in the newspapers each day.

We got diarrhea and upset stomachs from the unusual foods we chose from menus we couldn't read. One kind cook motioned us to the kitchen so we could point at foods like rice and peas that looked vaguely familiar. One evening tired little Matthew insisted, "I want a hamburger!" We almost never had hamburgers in the U.S., but after months of Kenyan *ugali* and now unfamiliar Turkish soups and stews, he wanted something "American."

One day on a language route that took him to a nearby Turkish tea house Richard met a young Turkish man who genuinely wanted to help. With the dictionary, broken English and Turkish, the man explained that Turkish apartments were not big enough to accommodate a family of five. But he had a rental flat, nearby, where we could stay, and he'd bring his family to meet our family.

As Richard was out on his language route, I was hunched over the tape recorder memorizing my text for the day. The children were restless in the one hotel room we shared, and the two boys asked if they could wrestle. I nodded my head without looking up.

A private bathroom adjoined our bedroom, separated by an opaque glass door. As they wrestled and I memorized my Turkish text, a loud crash brought the lesson to an end. The wrestling boys had fallen and pushed each other through the thick glass bathroom door. There was no blood, but were we pushing our children too hard? Ruining them? Four weeks living together in a hotel room. No school. Few books. Relentless Turkish study. Daily walks on cobblestone streets under overcast January skies.

One day as we walked the narrow streets lined with small shops selling fresh vegetables, dried nuts, meat, fresh bread, and canned goods, little Matthew accidentally knocked against a stack of crates filled with empty milk bottles. The crate tipped and the bottles spilled out to rattle over the cobblestones. The grocer shook his fist and yelled something we couldn't understand.

We stopped to help pick up the bottles. Then I realized I didn't even know how to say, "I'm sorry. It was an accident," in Turkish.

I came before the Lord asking for reassurance, and as I prayed that morning, I saw an unusual vision in my mind's eye. Years ago, I'd been intrigued by the model of a full-rigged sailing ship displayed inside a narrow-necked bottle sitting on a fireplace mantle.

Now I saw a narrow-necked bottle, but instead of a ship inside, I saw a big black Bible with gilt edged pages. How did the Bible get inside the bottle? I wondered. The only way to physically get a Bible inside a bottle would be to tear it apart, stuff it inside page by page.

In a flash I saw this unusual image as a parable of our entry into Turkey. We were being stuffed down the narrow neck of Turkish culture. It felt like we were being pulled apart and destroyed in the process. But the Spirit whispered, "I am placing you inside Turkish culture. It's unnatural. It's difficult. But when I do something, it is whole. It is complete. It is beautiful."

And that's exactly what we saw happening. Richard got a good job teaching English at Marmara University. We enrolled our children in the local Turkish elementary school. Curious children swarmed into our fifth floor flat, inviting our children out into the street for jump rope, tag, soccer. Women invited me to neighborhood tea and "work on your own handwork" gatherings. When they asked me what my handwork was, I'd hold up a dictionary and notepad. As they chatted and drank tea, I plied them with questions, using the opportunity to learn and practice Turkish.

"What color is the yarn? How many children do you have? Where do you live? What is that? Do you like tea?"

One Saturday an enthusiastic group of children showed up inviting our children to the movies. "What's showing," I asked. We didn't go to many movies as a family or even have a TV in the U.S., although we got one in Turkey to help with language learning. The one channel ran until midnight controlling the national bedtime. Dinner guests stayed until the TV went off air, not wanting to miss anything important.

The Turkish kids said the movie was *"Canavar! Canavar!"* That sounded like Joan of Arc. Maybe it would be a nice historical movie. Off they went. "Mom, it was horrible," Chad said and that's when I learned *canavar* was the Turkish word for monster.

The more we understood about Turkey and the Muslim friends we were making, the more we were impressed by the sincerity and devotion of many. Most had never met another Christian and were full of curious questions. Do Christians fast? How do you pray? We respect your prophet Jesus. Why don't you respect our Prophet Mohammed?

As they observed our family dressing modestly, not smoking or drinking, praying before meals and at family worship times, they wondered if we were Muslims. We weren't anything like the glamorous partying stars of *Dallas* or *Dynasty* that made their way to Turkish television presenting a picture of highflying life in "Christian" America.

We didn't have a host family, but an older widow who lived across the hall with her two young-adult children became an important language and culture teacher. She took me to street bazaars and helped bargain for fresh fruits and vegetables. She taught me how to cook Turkish food.

But we craved American foods too, so on Rhoda's tenth birthday, after we'd been in Turkey for eight months, we decided to introduce a whole tableful of neighborhood children to pizza. We bought bread dough from the local bakery and pressed it out on round trays then topped it with homemade pizza sauce, fried hamburger and a mild local cheese that resembled mozzarella. At the last minute I garnished the pizza with a few slices from a roll of German sausage a visiting friend had given.

The kids loved the homemade pizza––a food which had not yet found its way to Turkey. As they chattered away talking about how good it was I remarked that I'd topped it with some German sausage. Suddenly one of the girls froze, her hand halfway to her mouth with her second slice of pizza. "Does it have pig meat on it?" she asked, horrified.

"No," I said, too confidently. "Not all German sausage is made from pig meat." The children went back to eating, and I never went to the wastebasket to retrieve the label to read the ingredients. I didn't want to know that I could so easily have destroyed our budding friendships in the neighborhood.

By the time school started in the fall our children had learned enough street Turkish to navigate the local Turkish elementary and middle schools. We learned that for part of their studies they'd need to take Muslim religious education classes. After dropping them off at school Richard and I fell to our knees in the tiny living room that also served as our bedroom. We again gave our children to God, praying for his protection and wisdom.

Our children were minor celebrities. Classmates helped with homework. Rhoda joined a folk dancing group that performed in the national Children's Day festivities. Chad earned a few *lira* selling shopping bags at the bazaar with his friend. We had many friends in the neighborhood. One lady was concerned about who our children played with. She said they were learning crude, street Turkish and even swearing.

Then our Turkish bachelor friend came to visit. He's the one who had found us the fifth-floor flat that belonged to his family and helped us get settled. Now he told us we'd have to move out in the spring. One of his family members needed the flat. It was a logical request from a kind friend, but we hated to think of relocating for the last two months of the school year.

Daughter Rhoda, right, joined a Turkish folk dancing team.

A foreign family on the European side of the city who were going on home leave offered us their furnished basement flat for the few months we needed a place. We were planning to move to the southeastern city of Gaziantep for the next school year. We began the inevitable packing and preparation for moving once again.

I got the children off to their old school for the day, ran several bags of discarded clothing and broken toys down the five flights of stairs to the streetside garbage pile, and came back up to await the moving van we'd engaged to transport our belongings to the other side of the Bosphorus strait that divided Istanbul into European and Asian sides.

My eyes filled with tears of anger and self-pity. "Why do we have to move yet again? It's too much!" I prayed.

Then I noticed an old village woman wearing a flowered scarf and baggy shalwar trousers. She was pawing through the garbage and even though I was five stories up I could see the evident delight on her face when she discovered our children's broken toys. She stuffed our discarded belongings into her baggy shalwar pockets.

"Do you see the joy and gratitude in the heart of that old woman for some old, broken toys?" the Spirit whispered. "She doesn't even know me. You are my child. Can you trust me to work for good in this move?"

During those two months in our temporary housing on the European side of the Bosphorus, we became lifelong friends of a married couple who lived nearby. They were really struggling in their marriage. One day after we spent a precious time of counseling and prayer, I sensed God saying, "Do you see why I might have wanted you in this neighborhood?"

As my eyes clouded with tears I whispered, "When will I ever learn to trust you, God, to know that You are working for good in all things? Not my petty, self-centered good, but your eternal good that knows not time nor place. Thanks for occasionally pulling back the curtains to give us earthlings encouraging glimpses of your grand and glorious purposes."

Matthew beginning school in Istanbul, Turkey.

17

Gaziantep and the Southeast

Christmas with Gaziantep house church; Turkish guest in center, Rhoda and Chad.

As our RMM team met weekly for fellowship and prayer we prayed diligently that God would lead us to Turkish "Corneliuses" even as we asked God to prepare us with the insight and vision we needed to reach God-fearing Muslims who had not yet heard of Jesus.

Acts 10 tells the story of the Roman centurion, Cornelius, who was "devout and God-fearing," the first Gentile to receive the gift of the Holy Spirit along with his household. We knew there were thousands of "devout and God-fearing" Turks. We prayed for divine connections.

The year was 1983. There were Christian professionals living in Turkey's four largest cities, Istanbul, Ankara, Izmir, and Adana. But no one had ventured as far east as Gaziantep. There were fears of Turkish-Kurdish conflicts, earthquakes, and other unknowns. At one time Antep (short form of city name) had been home to a large Armenian population, but in 1915, the chaos and war in the disintegrating Ottoman Empire led to ethnic cleansing and genocide.

On an exploratory trip, Richard and two other team members got English teaching jobs at the Middle East Technical University, and we made plans to move. We engaged a truck to haul our belongings. Richard planned to travel with the truck, and the children and I would follow by bus. It was a new city, and we weren't exactly sure how we'd find each other when we arrived.

The huge lorry arrived, backing up to our tiny basement flat. It didn't take long to load our meager possessions into the front half of the truck bed. Then as we began to say our good-byes Richard suggested, "Why don't we all just ride in the back of the lorry? There's plenty of room."

And just like that we unrolled our carpets and sleeping mats in the truck bed, vaulted up, and were off. Outside the city, the star-studded sky shone clear and crisp. The smell of sheep and manure grew stronger as we nestled down for the night. I noticed swatches of sheep wool caught in the rough wooden sides of the truck. "Sheep led to the slaughter" had filled this truck before we did.

Our biggest problem was having no way to communicate with the drivers as they drove through the night without bathroom breaks. A few utensils from our kitchen wares served as pee pots until the first stop of the morning found us east of Ankara and well on our way to our new home.

This truck and two chauffeurs moved us and our few belongings to Gaziantep, Turkey.

We arrived in the early morning hours of the second day, waiting until daylight to unpack our belongings and settle into our new home, a three-bedroom, first-floor flat. We'd rented the flat on an earlier visit to the city. People were eager to assist. They assumed we were Christians since we were Americans.

Did we want to live in the Armenian quarter, still recognized as such? There was an American hospital, begun by missionaries among the Armenians in 1879. Those early missionaries had orchestrated the planting of thousands of trees that helped bring cooler temperatures and increased rainfall of this semi-arid region. Did we know of an American nurse who could work at the hospital and help raise the quality of care?

The staff and faculty at the university were welcoming, glad to have native speakers on staff to prepare entering students to study engineering in English. As far as we knew we were the only Americans and Christians in the large southeastern city of 600,000. Our team included another family and a single woman.

Interested friends told us there was no church in town and wondered where we'd worship. Old Armenian churches had been turned into prisons and town halls.

Our children started new schools. We began to meet the neighbors. Every Sunday afternoon we met as a team for Bible study and worship, praying that God would bring "Cornelius" to us.

While in Istanbul we'd learned of a Bible correspondence course that ran ads in national newspapers. Hundreds of curious Turks enrolled in the program. Those who worked their way successfully through the course, could request a Bible and eventually a visit from a Christian. Before coming to Antep, we agreed to follow up Bible course participants "from the east" who'd requested a visit from a Christian.

During the 1984 Christmas season someone from the Bible correspondence course in Istanbul came to visit, bringing with him a Turkish seeker from Antep.

We were still studying Turkish, beginning to read haltingly from several gospel portions that had been translated into more contemporary Turkish. But we'd never prayed in Turkish. Word was getting out that we had a worship service in our home Sunday afternoons. Curious students and other friends asked if they could visit since they'd never seen a Bible or been inside a church. We always told people they were welcome but doubted that they'd come.

Then one Sunday afternoon the doorbell rang. And it rang again. I fled into the kitchen to put on the water for tea. The doorbell rang again. When everyone had gathered there were seven Turks in the living room, and none of them spoke English.

"What are we going to do?" I prayed in a panic. Of course, we'd hoped to have Turks join our fellowship but after we'd learned a little more Turkish. "We aren't ready," I told God.

"What can you say?" Jesus asked. "Can you say five words and two sentences? Just give me what you have—like the little Galilean boy with his lunch—and watch me feed the multitudes."

I picked up my double-decker teapot and tray of tulip tea glasses on tiny silver saucers. I served the guests in the living room. I sat on the floor and cracked pistachio nuts to share. (Antep was known as "the pistachio nut capital of the world.")

One man there that day could not stop smiling and staring at us. He's the one who had completed the Bible correspondence course and requested a visit from a Christian. His story poured out. When he was eight years old he'd heard stories from the Bible shared by some Italian engineers who'd worked with his dad to install the electrical grid for the city. The Bible stories had gripped his heart and changed his identity. He began to tell people he was not a Muslim, but people laughed at him. "All Turks are Muslims," they said. The "Christian" Greeks and Armenians had been driven out. To be Turkish was to be Muslim. Ethnicity and religion were seamless.

As he grew older, he tried to find a Bible or meet a Christian so he could learn more about Jesus. He even travelled to Germany and visited a cathedral. As he sat in the back, he said, the most wonderful peace in the world came over him. He sensed God saying, "Those who seek me will find me."

Now Christians had moved to his home city. He was so glad to be near other Christians, he told us later, he used to walk past our apartment so he could feel near other Christians for the first time in his life. He didn't want to appear too eager and drive us away. Later he brought his wife and two young children. He invited us to his home and pointed to the picture of a German cathedral on his living room wall. It was the first place he'd sensed the true presence of God.

When this couple and another single woman, a student at the university, requested baptism we planned a picnic on a Mediterranean beach several hours drive away. Our oldest son Chad was also part of that baptismal celebration and swim-picnic on the beach.

Several non-believers were part of the group. On the surface this outing was a beach picnic. One couple who went along were neighbors of the newly believing Turkish couple. They owned the minibus that transported us. Because of the presence of the chauffer couple, another relative, and the sensitivity of baptizing Muslim converts to Christianity, our conversations along the way were generic and surfacy.

On the way home the young wife—fresh from the baptismal waters—led out in a joyful song, "The old Adam is buried; the new Adam is resurrected!" Tentatively at first, then exuberantly we all joined in as she led one worship song after another. The rented minibus could not contain the joy.

I was sitting in front, right behind the Muslim minibus driver and his wife. As the songs swelled around us, I gave them a worried glance. The wife leaned over to her chauffer husband and said wistfully, "I wish our religion had songs in it."

Another university student who had been attending our Sunday afternoon worship gatherings left for the summer, then came for a visit when school resumed in the fall. He was eager to share about his momentous summer.

His amazing story tumbled out. He'd started coming to our housechurch pretending to be a believer. But really, he was an infiltrator, a member of a right-wing Islamic group that hated what we were doing. He'd figured out we were "missionaries," and thought he'd learn of our activities to turn us into the authorities.

But then he became intrigued by our lives and the stories of Jesus we read together. He remembered the first Sunday he visited—how we humbly sat on the floor and served our guests tea and pistachios. We were educated Americans, his social superiors, why were we serving him and other students so humbly? He sensed a different Spirit in our home. On one level, he hated everything we stood for, but he said, "There was a strange Spirit in your house. It kept drawing me back."

During the summer he'd painted houses in the hot sun. One day he returned from work with a bad headache and grabbed a pill from the medicine cabinet. Almost immediately his throat began to swell shut. He gasped for breath and fell onto the bed. He knew he must be suffering severe allergic reactions to the medication. Fearing for his life, he suddenly remembered the stories of Jesus we'd read together. He cried out, "Jesus, heal me!" Instantly he could breathe again and fell into a peaceful sleep.

Several weeks later he was with friends at a party. The blaring music brought on a headache, so he asked the hostess for a pain pill. As his body again went into a severe allergic reaction friends rushed him to the hospital. Doctors administered an antidote and warned him never to take that drug again. They said the reaction was life-threatening and would not go away without medication.

That's when he knew that Jesus had touched him miraculously the first time. He wanted to follow Jesus, to be filled with his Spirit. He danced around the yard, singing and praying. Then he looked at me, "It all started that first day when you sat on the floor and cracked pistachios for me." He asked to be baptized in our bathtub.

Others came too. Several young seekers had travelled to the nearest Catholic church several hours away, seeking Christian instruction. When they learned of our presence in their city they began attending the Sunday fellowship.

One young man had found a Bible, wrapped in brown paper, hidden on a high shelf in the store where he worked. He began reading in Matthew and was startled to see the words of Jesus admonishing his followers to "love your enemies." No human would ever say something that radical. It had to be the words of the true God.

Another read both the Koran and the Bible, seeking truth. He opened the two books on the table in front of him and prayed fervently that God would show him which was the true Word of God. As he prayed a ball of light came out of the right corner of the room and shimmered on the pages of the Bible.

The Christian couple who had been baptized at the beach lived in a compound with their extended family. The families each had their own living spaces but shared a central courtyard for joint work.

This couple often invited us to their home for worship and fellowship. They took out a wall to enlarge a room for meetings. One Sunday we noticed more attenders than usual. We all sat around on the brightly colored kilims and carpets. Some of the courtyard relatives were visiting.

They were eager to tell us what had happened the night before. Their small nephew had become deathly ill during the night. The concerned parents gathered beside his feverish body chanting memorized Arabic prayers and invoking the help of Muslim saints.

As the terrified parents watched, their young son went into convulsions. Suddenly they remembered the Jesus their brother had been telling them about, a Jesus who loves, forgives, and heals. This idea was strange and foreign, but in desperation they cried out to Jesus to heal their son. Instantly the convulsions stopped. The fever broke, and the little boy fell into a peaceful sleep.

Now the whole courtyard wanted to know more about this Jesus.

As more people became interested, we heard rumors that the police were watching us, asking people about us, investigating our activities. We weren't doing anything illegal. The Turkish constitution promised freedom of religion, but we also knew that although it was not illegal to change one's religion from Muslim to Christian, it was unacceptable.

I wondered if Richard missed the preaching he'd frequently done before coming to Turkey. Here there was no visible church, no pulpit, only a house church, home Bible studies, and an English classroom.

One day after returning from the university he commented offhandedly, "When I'm in front of the classroom teaching English, I feel like I'm preaching."

"He's really popular with the students," a coworker said. "After class they all swarm around him like bees to honey."

The students didn't know it, but they were being drawn to Jesus. Jesus made English attractive. Just our being present in Gaziantep was giving students the opportunity to know Jesus. We plant and water, but the Spirit gives life to the seed. Then I remembered the words of Paul who had travelled these very same roads in the first century. *"How can they believe in the one of whom they have not heard? And how can they hear without someone preaching to them?"* (Romans 10:14)

One weekend Richard went to Malatya to visit a man who had completed the Bible correspondence course based in Istanbul. He'd requested a visit from a believer and even though Malatya was five hours away from Antep by bus, we were the nearest known believers.

Although he didn't know it at the time, somewhere along the way, the secret police began trailing Richard as he made his way to visit the isolated believer in Malatya.

After a warm visit the Turkish believer escorted Richard back to the bus station. As they waited for the bus, Richard noticed two men in black trench coats coming through the lounge checking everyone's passports. They checked Richard's passport and asked him to come with them to the police station along with the Turkish believer.

Richard spent the next two days under house arrest, not able to contact anyone. His interrogator's job was to find out why he'd come to Malatya and why he was living in Gaziantep. No generic answers would do. The interrogator wanted to know how he knew the man he was visiting. What were the names of other Christians in the southeast?

As the threats escalated—"You know I could put you six feet under,"—Richard sensed the Spirit saying, "Tell him everything about yourself, but nothing about anyone else."

Surprisingly the interrogator agreed to those conditions. Richard began in Kentucky and shared the story of his life, how he'd met the Lord and came to Turkey because we sensed that's what God was calling us to do.

The interrogator could not understand spiritual motivation. Surely Richard was in the pay of the U.S. government, receiving a monetary reward for each Turkish convert.

Back in Gaziantep we gathered for supper without Richard. He was planning to be there and had a rendezvous planned with a visiting mission administrator. I tucked the children in bed for the night. They cried and asked, "Where's Daddy?"

"I don't know," I answered. "But God knows. We can trust Daddy to Him."

Something was not right. A bus accident, flood, or earthquake? We didn't have a phone but used the neighbor's phone as an emergency contact. If Richard could have called, he would have. I knew he would not casually miss the Turkish fellowship he was planning to lead the following afternoon in our home.

I slept fitfully that night, straining to hear the clink of the key in the latch. I woke with the words of an old hymn coursing through my mind:

Like a river glorious is God's perfect peace, over all victorious in its bright increase;
Perfect, yet it floweth fuller every day. Perfect, yet it groweth deeper all the way.

Stayed upon Jehovah hearts are fully blessed. Finding as He promised, perfect peace and rest.

Every joy or trial falleth from above, traced upon our dial by the Sun of Love.
We may trust Him fully all for us to do; they who trust him wholly find Him wholly true.

I remembered that I'd given my husband to God back in California, when I thought he'd die of cancer. He was God's. We were God's. Our times were in his hand.

The rainy spring Sunday moved slowly. Guests showed up for afternoon fellowship. We drank tea and ate *katmer,* a paper-thin pastry stuffed with pistachios, honey, and clotted cream. I invited one of the Turkish believers to lead our time together. We sang softly. We prayed for Richard and the other unknowns in all our lives. Several shared that the secret police had recently questioned them about our activities.

The Turkish guests left. The next day the children had school. Richard was scheduled to teach at the university. I tucked the children in for the second night—not knowing where their father was. The last bus from Malatya would arrive before midnight. I'd wait for that. Then maybe I should call someone? Report a missing person? But who? My parents? Our sending team back in Rosedale? The U.S. Embassy?

Then I heard the most welcome sound I could imagine—the rattle of the key in the lock. I flew to the door and into Richard's weary arms. His story tumbled out. He'd just spent 48 intense hours in custody. The Turkish authorities were investigating us and our activities.

The next day the university fired him and our other teammate. That was a disappointing blow, but then we learned of the need for a bilingual translator at a large pistachio nut import-export company. Richard got the job, a good salary, and work permit. We could stay for the time being anyway, but surveillance and investigation ramped up. Believers and seekers, students and friends were called in for questioning.

The Turkish constitution guaranteed freedom of religion, but it was illegal to "use religion for personal gain." That was the charge leveled against us.

Interest continued growing. We enrolled our children in school for another year. Our fledgling fellowship was rich and sweet. We often spent Sunday afternoons sitting together on the floor drinking endless glasses of tea and eating *cig kofte,* a local delicacy made of kneading together finely ground raw lamb, wheat bulgar, pepper paste, olive oil, and chopped parsley.

When I said I wasn't sure I wanted to eat raw meat our host laughed and said it wasn't raw. The heat of his hands cooked it as he kneaded. Or maybe there'd be charbroiled kebabs over pilav, red lentil soup with fresh bread, *lamachun.* a pizza-type flat bread topped with finely chopped parsley, onions and tomatoes, or stuffed eggplant and peppers.

One day the women of the extended family of several of the believers invited me to help them make a winter's supply of flat village bread. They'd roll the dough made of freshly ground whole wheat flour and water into large, thin sheets, toast it until brown-flecked and crisp on a round griddle, then place the baked bread discs in a covered stack.

When they wanted fresh bread for a kebab sandwich or to scoop up stew, they'd sprinkle the dry bread discs with water until they became soft and pliable.

For this huge operation the women sat on the floor in front of little round tables about 12 inches high. With long thin rolling pins about the size of a broom handle, they'd roll the hunks of dough into perfect circles about 20 inches in diameter.

They worked quickly, deftly flicking their wrists as they flattened the dough and stacked it for drying. Didn't I want to try, they wondered. They'd been doing this since they were eight years old.

I sat down gingerly, trying to do what they did. My bread was lumpy, uneven and soon developed a jagged hole in the middle. The women gathered around, laughing at my efforts. It's child's work, they joked, shooing me away to watch as they kept up their momentum.

They talked fast in a village dialect I couldn't follow very well. They laughed in good fun. I was the day's entertainment, an adult woman who didn't even know how to make simple village bread.

I felt out of place, like I didn't belong. Why did we even come to Turkey? I'll never fit in here, I mused. I'm just a clumsy, tongue-tied child.

"You are a child, my child," the Holy Spirit spoke into my self-pity. "I'm glad you came, and I liked your bread!"

Our little house fellowship was beginning to learn about life together. One believer persuaded another to co-sign for a new TV. Trust was being built among people of different ethnic groups, economic and social standings.

Then the needy believer sold the TV, used the money to pay his debts, and did not repay the co-signer; a wife left her husband, upset by his irresponsibility. A young believer fell into suicidal depression. Another had medical needs––a huge tumor on his neck––without the resources to get medical attention. Believers' children were teased at school and called "infidels." Questions about Islamic circumcision arose. Do Christians circumcise their sons? We studied the scriptures together. We worshipped.

These new believers had never been to an organized church. One gray winter Sunday as we sang a joyful song about Jesus, the light of the world, a young woman leaped to her feet, switched on the light, and led us in a circle dance.

We saw miracles. After evening prayer, the neck tumor burst and drained completely away. Forgiveness was asked and received. A university student threw away his cigarettes and attracted the attention of other incredulous students who also wanted to quit.

One man noticed our family's dishwashing schedule tacked on the refrigerator. He was surprised we all took turns—even Richard. "Christian men work in the kitchen?" He turned to his wife with a grin. "We need to do that too."

One of the new believers invited us to visit his friend. As we listened, the believer shared his testimony with his friend. "How can a Muslim become a Christian?" the seeker wondered. He liked what he heard about Jesus. The Bible was an amazing book. Mohammed even said they should read it. But there is such a huge gulf between Muslims and Christians. "How can Jesus be the Son of God, and how did you change your religion?" he asked.

The Turkish believer opened his Bible to Matthew 16:17, and read Jesus' words to Peter, "Flesh and blood did not reveal this to me," he grinned at us. "It wasn't them," he said, then continued reading, "but my Father who is in heaven." We continued to pray for revelation.

Light was breaking through the darkness.

Richard was regularly summoned to the police station for questioning. But the chief investigator's children went to school with our children. They wondered if I could teach English at the school. Hopeful signs.

One day Rhoda came home from school saying that in religion class she'd been assigned to give a speech on why Mohammed is a superior prophet to Jesus. When I learned that the topics had been assigned randomly, I suggested she ask her teacher if she could speak on something else. The teacher gladly agreed to change her topic and suggested she give a speech to the class explaining what Christians believe.

I remembered our anguished prayers when we'd first sent our children away to Turkish schools, knowing they'd need to take the compulsory religion classes.

Matthew was always busy with a troupe of little boys, trying to find spots to play soccer. Most green areas had "keep off the grass" signs, but the boys would play until a grumpy, half-sleeping guard would chase them off.

Our kind neighbor, a doctor's wife from across the hall, would cluck her tongue, and say, "Lider, lider," marveling at the way Matthew always drew a crowd.

Then one quiet October afternoon, I answered a knock on our first-floor apartment door. A policeman stood there. He handed me a paper and said that our passports had been revoked. We would need to leave the country within 48 hours and never return.

We lived an 18-hour bus ride away from the nearest international airport. So we appealed for more time to dismantle our household and make our exit. We were granted a week.

On hearing the news, the neighbors and believers gathered to assist and grieve our departure. One man took on the job of selling our large household furnishings. Smaller things we gave away. My neighbor and I had just made a large plastic barrel full of pickled cucumbers and cabbage for the winter. She sadly took it away to share with other neighbors.

When the children came home from school, they saw the house in disarray with stacks of things to be packed or disposed of. I sent Rhoda off to pack up her room, only to learn later that in this traumatic, grief-filled moment, she knelt by the bed, committing her life to carry on the unfinished work we were being forced to abandon.

Chad began high school attending Anadolu Lisesi in Gaziantep.

A university student we'd baptized in our bathtub came to help with evening packing the last night we slept there. Late that evening he knelt at the door to put on his shoes before going out into the night. He looked up at me as tears rolled down my cheeks. It felt like we were parents being torn prematurely from young children.

"Jewel," he said, "Just remember, someday every knee will bow, and every tongue confess that Jesus Christ is Lord, to the glory of God the Father."

He disappeared into the night, but I knew he knew. The light was shining in the darkness.

We gathered for a last prayer time before catching the overnight bus. We cried and clung to one another, building an altar of sodden tissues in the middle of the Turkish carpet.

On the long bus ride west across the Anatolian highlands to Istanbul, I sat by the window filled with questions. We were just beginning to know the language. Our children had friends. The little fellowship was growing in size and maturity. We had hoped to stay for at least 10 years to see a strong, reproducing indigenous church emerge.

As I pressed my nose against the cold glass of the bus window, I noticed a full golden moon lighting up the rock-strewn countryside. Then as I watched in horror, a thick, black shadow crept across the moon face, completely blotting out the light. A lunar eclipse.

For the next hours as I watched, the darkness blotted out the light, then slowly receded. And the moon was back.

Into my grief, the Spirit whispered, "Darkness is only temporary. Light wins!"

18

Turkish Republic of North Cyprus

We arrived back in Ohio without home, job, car, or credit. Suddenly what we had thought God was calling us to give our lives to was no longer an option. We struggled to survive and understand what God had for us in this next season.

The first Sunday back at the Mechanicsburg Christian Fellowship God gave us a special word about "dormancy." We must not discount the dark days of winter. Just as he prepares peach trees for an abundant crop through the cold stillness of winter, he would use this time of "dormancy" in our lives. Dormancy is a necessary part of fruit bearing.

I remembered the peach orchards of my childhood in Virginia, the vulnerable pink blossoms of spring that heralded a crop of peaches. I prayed for the patience to lie dormant, to understand this death of a vision to which we'd given all we had, but it wasn't easy.

My mother-in-law, Rhoda Showalter, who was the women's matron at RBC, invited me to speak to the women students one evening. As I looked out on the fresh young faces upturned with hope and vision, I was raw with grief and disillusionment.

214 | JEWEL SHOWALTER

I felt like saying, "Some of you want to get married, but you never will. Some of you will get married, but you'll be barren. Some of you will get divorced, or your husband will die a cruel, lingering death. Your child might be stillborn or get hit by a car. You might go bankrupt. Life just doesn't work out like you think it should!"

Somehow I managed to say something blandly inspirational and inoffensive without breaking into tears.

We bought a car which I soon wrecked in an icy slide through a red light. Stores refused to cash our checks because we had no jobs or credit. Our children jumped back into school at Shekinah Christian School. Richard contracted drywall jobs. I began work as a copy editor at the RMM office in exchange for rent on one of their empty apartments. Slowly we began to heal and understand what might come next.

Richard took an exploratory trip to visit other Turkish immigrant communities in Germany and north Cyprus. He learned he could cross into Turkey as a tourist without any problems. After a visit to the Turkish Republic of North Cyprus, an easy ferry boat ride from the Turkish mainland, we began to sense that this may be the next right step and a continuation of Turkish ministry.

As we prepared to move to north Cyprus for a new season of ministry, Rhoda and Matthew were not excited about leaving Ohio. In fact, 16-year-old Rhoda was exerting her independence, all but refusing to return with us. We'd given Chad the opportunity of remaining in the U.S., why couldn't she?

We continued to feel she should go back with us but didn't want to force her. When she returned from a week at Bethel Camp, shortly before we were scheduled to leave for Cyprus, Rhoda was a changed young woman. "God is calling me as a missionary to Cyprus," she said with a tear-stained smile.

Richard and I, with our two younger children, drove toward Pennsylvania where he'd fly to California for his brother's wedding while Rhoda, Matt, and I spent a few days with my Wenger family. Then we'd rendezvous in New York for our flight together to a new life and ministry in Cyprus.

After church in Lancaster, Pennsylvania, my parents loaded their station wagon with our eight large suitcases and began the 3½ hour drive to JFK International Airport where we planned to meet Richard. About an hour from the airport, our back wheels began to make a strange rattling noise that grew increasingly louder. My father pulled to the berm, afraid that his wheel bearings were going out and he wouldn't be able to safely continue the trip.

As we waited on the shoulder of the highway, an airport limousine stopped and asked if we needed help. He had room for two passengers but not our eight suitcases. We called a taxi from the neighboring town. I quickly decided I'd have to send the children in the limo and take the luggage by myself in the taxi hoping we'd all arrive at the same place around the same time.

My parents' car was stranded. The limo couldn't wait. The taxi arrived—a battered, black vehicle with a large trunk. The young driver flung back his dreads, named his price and hobbled over to load our luggage in his cavernous trunk. My parents paid both the limo and taxi drivers with money left in their cash box from their previous day on Central Market.

I tried to shove Rhoda and Matt into the limo, but young Matt clung to me crying, refusing to be separated. Suddenly Rhoda stepped forward. "I'll go with the luggage," she said, and just that quick she was off with the dread-locked taxi driver while Matt and I squeezed into the limo.

"Meet you at the gate," I shouted, helpless, as the taxi sped off with Rhoda and the luggage, weaving back and forth through four lanes of traffic and soon lost from sight.

When the limo arrived at our JFK gate I saw, to my immense relief, a surprised Richard, who'd arrived on an earlier flight from California, greeting Rhoda as she and the luggage spilled onto the pavement. We grabbed our suitcases and dashed to check in just as the gate was about to close. We'd made it. Off to our new life as a family of four in north Cyprus.

It was the fall of 1987 and Richard had a job teaching English in the University of Girne (Kyrenia) on the north coast of Cyprus. We moved to the village of Catalkoy, just outside Girne, with a stunning view of the Mediterranean Sea to the north.

Chad was settled back into Shekinah Christian School glad he wouldn't have to adjust to yet another new country and school system. Two Ohio families, both with boys near his age, had offered to serve as host families for him. Our little family was experiencing our first separation.

I had vowed never to send my children to a missionary children's boarding school, but if the child preferred to stay in the U.S. rather than go overseas with the family, could this be part of a healthy separation, a growing up? It was time to allow him to make that choice.

Life in the Cypriot village was indeed another culture. Most residents of our village had been resettled from a Turkish village in the south during the ethnic unrest of the previous 20 years in which both Greeks and Turks battled for supremacy. The young republic, founded in 1983, is not recognized by the international community.

Our neighbors said they felt like they were living temporarily in borrowed homes. In a massive population exchange overseen by the U.N., the Greek residents in the north and the Turkish residents in the south had left their homes with only the clothes on their backs expecting to return, only to be resettled in comparable homes elsewhere without the possibility of ever going back. The Green Line, manned by the United Nations, kept the two ethnic groups apart, with no possibility of crossing over—even for foreigners.

Our Turkish neighbor pointed to the photos on the wall—those of the previous Greek owners who had been resettled in the south. He joked that he wasn't taking their photos down because someday they'd be back to reclaim their property. "My landlords," he said with a grin.

When we walked down for a swim in the Mediterranean, we rambled past what had been an elegant Greek villa. Inside the fence, a Turkish village family camped out, grazing their sheep on the lawn, planting eggplant, peppers, and tomatoes in the formerly landscaped flower beds.

We had arrived during the hot dry season, but when the spring rains fell, hundreds of brilliant pink cyclamen blooms carpeted the meadows and sprang from the rocky mountain craigs. The bulbs had been there all along, and we had never known.

Cyprus still used the British school system, different from the Turkish and American systems our children had already adjusted to.

This made home schooling an attractive option, although we'd never considered that before, wanting instead to be immersed in the life of the community.

We partnered with two other international couples who were already living on the island and made plans to begin an international church. Surprisingly our house fellowship quickly filled up with Iranians who were fleeing the regime change in Iran and found Cyprus a convenient stopping place on their way to find sanctuary in the west.

The sincerity and openness of the Iranians was surprising and refreshing. They were eager to read the Bible and hear the gospel for the first time. One man was skeptical at first. Shite Islam was all he'd ever known. Mohammed was his prophet, but he was curious and open.

One evening, sitting on our porch enjoying a glass of Turkish tea he said, "You know, when I started reading the New Testament, I saw Mohammed towering over your holy book. He was my prophet. But the more I read, the more Mohammed shrank. Jesus began to grow. I fell in love with Jesus, and then Mohammed just shriveled away." He requested baptism.

One evening in a group of Iranian believers and seekers a man asked, "Do any of you know who the most effective missionary to the Muslim world is?"

We waited curiously for his answer.

"It's the Ayatollah Khomeini," he proclaimed loudly, glancing over his shoulder. "He's showed us the true face of Islam. Islam unmasked. We see truly what it is, and we don't want it!"

Other Turkish seekers came forward to join the fellowship. We also met regularly with an extended family in a mountain village—catching an evening bus into their village, overnighting in their home for an evening of fellowship, and returning on the one bus out of the village in the morning.

One evening after I caught a minibus to Girne and walked to the village bus station to catch the bus into the village for our overnight fellowship, I was drenched in a torrential rainstorm. I waded through water up to my ankles, beginning to grumble about my wet feet. Suddenly I remembered Jesus washing the feet of his disciples and urging them to serve one another. "How else will the gospel reach the remote villages of north Cyprus?" the Spirit whispered. "Your feet are beautiful!"

Groves of olive trees covered the island in all directions. Many of our neighbors were small farmers who harvested the olives by hand, saving a few crocks full to preserve in a salty brine for eating but hauling the bulk of the crop to the olive press in the village.

We helped with the harvest. Beating the trees with broom sticks, so the green and black olives rained down on drop cloths to be dumped into large burlap sacks.

I loved watching the olive press at work. After farmers dumped their sacks of hard fresh olives into a circular stone trough, the miller turned on a large, electric-powered millstone that whirled over the olives, pulverizing them into a gray-green mash. Then the miller shoveled the olive mash into specially woven goat hair pouches about a foot square. He stacked the pouches 10-15 high and squeezed the stack with a hydraulic press. The sides of the stack glistened as oil and water filtered out through the pouches to trickle down and into a trough that funneled the precious liquid into a large centrifuge. As the liquid swirled in a huge vat you could see the virgin olive oil rising to the top, separated from the black bitter water.

The farmer brought his own flasks and cans to fill with the golden liquid while the black bitter water—good for nothing—spilled out onto the cobblestone streets and drained away.

The olive press preached a sermon as I watched, transfixed. How like the hard, bitter olives we humans are. But when we submit to the crushing, squeezing, swirling of the olive press, a valuable oil is released. An oil that is used for food, light, perfume, healing, anointing.

When we get rid of our black bitter water, God can use us to bring food to the hungry and serve up the Bread of Life. Our oil can fill the oil lamps of those who sit in darkness. When oil is mixed with aromatic spices it becomes a "fragrant aroma" in putrid places. Oil brings healing when poured on wounds. It calms troubled waters. Oil anoints us for the priestly duty of representing God on earth, announcing his kingdom where the god of this world still holds sway.

We prayed this for the people of Cyprus and of Turkey. Richard continued making visits back to the little fellowship in Gaziantep. It was struggling but surviving.

At Christmas time Chad came for a visit. We reveled in being a complete family again. We took photos in front of bush-sized poinsettias, chopped off an evergreen sprig to decorate for a Christmas tree, made orange marmalade and lemon curd from the small orchard in our yard, introduced him to our friends.

Richard, Chad, and Matt took a cold, Christmas day swim in the little cove, a fifteen-minute walk down the hill from our village of Catalkoy. We sang Christmas carols and roasted chestnuts as we huddled around the fireplace, our only source of warmth during the cool, rainy evenings.

Then all too soon it was time for Chad to return to the U.S. Richard travelled with him by ferry to the Turkish mainland. In the enormous Adana bus station, Chad took a bus west to Istanbul to catch his return flight to Columbus, Ohio, and Richard took a bus headed east to visit the little believers' fellowship in Gaziantep.

That parting with Chad in the Adana bus station was one of the most difficult things Richard had ever done. Everything in him wanted to cling to his son, to travel with him to Istanbul and back to America, to watch his high school basketball games, and perhaps, meet his first girlfriend.

As his smoke-filled bus headed east carrying him ever further from his adolescent son, Richard argued with God. "Why can't I be like any other American dad—cheering on his son's team? It's too painful. The cost is too high. Why do we have to be separated like this?"

God's voice cut through the haze of the harsh Turkish tobacco smoke that filled the bus.

"It's because you have other sons. They need you now. I am with Chad. I love him more than you do." Richard buried his face in his hands and silently shook with sobs. Suddenly the bus felt like a burning bush.

Shortly after that visit we got a hurried call from one of the student believers. "Please pray for me," he said tersely. "The police are on campus looking for me." Then the line went dead.

A believing woman also called. "Please pray. They took my husband," she said.

For days we heard nothing, but the local newspapers told the story of how the government was investigating a growing movement of Turks from Muslim background who were calling themselves "Believers" or "Followers of Jesus." This term was being used to distinguish the growing Turkish Protestant church from the word "Christian," historically applied only to citizens who were ethnically Greek, Armenian, or Assyrian—"enemies" of the Turkish Republic.

This was a brand-new phenomenon. Turkish authorities had no framework for the emerging category of Turkish "Followers of Jesus." While there was freedom of religion in Turkey, to be Turkish was to be Muslim. "Turkish Christian" was an oxymoron.

All over Turkey, young Turkish believers and seekers, were arrested, interrogated, photographed—their stories and testimonies shared in the newspapers. The address to the Bible correspondence course was printed warning readers not to read the propaganda issuing from that box number. A copy of the Christian "sinners' prayer" was published with a warning.

Shortly thereafter the Bible correspondence course reported a huge spike in interest through the free publicity. Isolated believers all over Turkey felt a new camaraderie with far-flung believers they'd never met. One told me later that the slanderous reports encouraged him, and suddenly he didn't feel so alone.

Turkish believers in the more cosmopolitan west were called in for questioning and soon released, but two of the leading believers in Gaziantep were imprisoned and tortured even though this was illegal for Turkey, a member of NATO.

As we heard the news that trickled out, we called a special day of prayer and fasting for our team and other believers in north Cyprus. I'd prayed before, but never so fervently. We knelt, lay prostrate, sobbed, and groaned. The words of Jesus became flesh among us, "In this world you will have tribulation..." This was the closest to "tribulation" we'd ever come. These were our dear brothers and sisters in Christ. But Jesus didn't stop there. He added, "Be of good cheer, for I have overcome the world."

We prayed that our brothers and sisters would stand firm in their faith. We'd often heard stories of the torture Turkish police were famous for. We raised money and hired a lawyer. We notified the American embassy.

After a month in prison, both men were finally released. We travelled to the Turkish mainland to meet together. We arranged physical exams for them with a Christian Turkish doctor. We listened to their stories.

The student had been expelled from the university, not permitted to complete the last year of his engineering program. He was a shadow of his former self. While he reaffirmed his faith, he was discouraged that in some ways, like Peter, he'd denied his Lord.

He shared a particularly difficult day when he shivered on the cold, wet cement floor of his solitary cell after brutal interrogation. "Why do I have to suffer so?" he cried out to God in agony, and was surprised by the answering whisper, "So that other Turks will know that some Turks follow Jesus."

Of course, the student had not seen the national newspapers that splashed his photo across their front pages, lining him up in front of a table full of confiscated Bibles, Christian books, and tapes. This was the common pose used to portray terrorists who were arrested—posing them behind tables displaying their confiscated rifles and machine guns.

The intended message was clear—Christians are enemies of the state just as much as violent Kurdish separatists.

The married man and his wife shared their story. At first, he'd been very tough, refusing to cooperate with the interrogators. Then they brought in his wife and began beating her in front of him—threatening to go further if he didn't talk and supply the names of other Christians. They called him an infidel, derisively slapping on an Armenian nickname.

He'd lost 30 pounds and had begun smoking again. Because he was a civil servant, they couldn't fire him but stripped him of his good job in the city's water system and banished him to a low-level job in another city. Their children were being ridiculed at school.

As we listened to their pain, suffering, and ostracism, tears running down our cheeks, I wondered if they wished they'd never met us.

"I'm so sorry," I whispered, hugging my friend. "Maybe we shouldn't have come to your city. Your lives have really been turned upside down."

She looked back at me with fire in her eyes. "How can you say that? We've gained so much more than we ever lost."

Then she said, "Look at these verses I found." She opened the New Testament to Matthew 5:11-12 and read, "Blessed are you when people insult you, persecute you and falsely say all kinds of evil against you because of me. Rejoice and be glad, because great is your reward in heaven, for in the same way they persecuted the prophets who were before you."

"We're blessed by God," she said simply.

The student shared a vision he'd had while in prison. In the distance he saw a preacher speaking to a large crowd of people. As he came closer, he saw that the people flocking to hear the message were Turks. He wondered who the preacher was. He turned to Richard and said with a wry grin, "The preacher wasn't you. And it wasn't' me." Then his face took on a look of awe. "The preacher," he said, "was Jesus."

***

We returned to Ohio for the summer, processing a call from Rosedale Bible College for Richard to serve as the next president. He would succeed Walter Beachy, a well-loved pastor at United Bethel Mennonite Church, who had also been serving as president.

With one child on the cusp of adulthood and two others coming on fast, we sensed our time living overseas may be coming to an end. While the needs of the Turkish world tugged at our hearts, we also felt a need to root again among our people, our "tribe"—the churches that had sent and supported us.

We began our last trip to our Cyprus home in late summer of 1988 with only our youngest child, Matthew. The year would be filled with travel, wrapping up work in Cyprus, and turning things over to coworkers. Chad and Rhoda would stay with their grandparents, David and Rhoda Showalter and attend Shekinah Christian School until we returned in the spring.

As we drove to the airport Matt was in the back seat crying. He didn't want to leave Ohio. Once again, we'd said goodbye to close friends and family—this time his two older siblings.

Would our lives always include so many painful goodbyes? I was good at hiding the pain of partings. Hadn't I been doing that all of my life? Just swallow the tears and set my face toward the new challenge. But Richard pulled the car to the side of the road and asked me to drive. As I took the wheel, he climbed into the back seat, put his arm around little Matt's shaking shoulders and cried with him.

When we put our "hand to the plow" at the invitation of Jesus, he says we shouldn't look back. But he doesn't say we won't wet the plow handle with our tears.

19

Rosedale Bible College

Al and Cathy Troyer, dear friends and part of the early MCF church planting team, came to us and said that God had told them to build us a house in Rosedale. We were awed and humbled. Of course, we'd need somewhere to live. We'd lodged in all sorts of places. We'd never had a "dream house."

Jesus tells his followers to, "Seek first the Kingdom of God and his righteousness, and all these things (houses, lands, food, clothing) will be added..."

So now when someone was offering to build us a house, what kind of a house did we even want? Here in the U.S. most people's garages were bigger than many homes in other places we'd lived. For sure we wouldn't need a garage. And we'd like a small apartment on one end so we could care for elderly parents, house young adults in transition, or move there ourselves someday. The things we'd come to value found their way into our building plans.

Al Troyer managed the project, and volunteers from the church and community helped with a "house frolic" to frame up the modest two-story Cape Cod on five acres just outside Rosedale. Richard did the drywall. Others assisted with cabinets, trim, plumbing, and electrical work.

We'd never had to mow lawns or look after flower beds before. One day as I spent several hours weeding and landscaping the lawn I remembered the hundreds of Turkish villages we'd bussed past on the 18 hours it took from Gaziantep in the southeast to Istanbul. "How will those people ever hear of you, Jesus?" I cried. "Is this really how you want us to be spending our time?"

We spoke at a Thanksgiving banquet in a large fancy restaurant. I made small talk with the woman beside me asking what she liked to do. She said she liked to shop. She's always on the look-out for bargain, name-brand clothes for her grandkids. And she liked to go out to eat with friends. She even organized a group to travel eight hours to another region with good shopping outlets and restaurants. Oh, and she loved redecorating her home too. Trying out new colors. New curtains and blinds.

I felt like screaming. Lady, do you know that I've just come from a country where most people never even met a Christian? You probably drive past three to four churches to get to **your** church. But did you know that in Turkey you can drive hundreds of miles and never pass a church of any kind?

Did I belong here? Could I fit in? And now that we were back, how could I challenge women to be involved in ministry rather than in malls? To be pouring out their prayers rather than their pocketbooks?

We were living in an era and place of great privilege and opportunity. How could we serve here? The Apostle Paul speaks of "learning the secret of living with plenty and with want." For this season we were living with "plenty."

The Sunday after we moved into our spacious new house I was overwhelmed with gratitude. I hugged Al. "Thank you so much!" I cried into his shoulder. "I never ever thought I'd live in a new house."

He looked back at me with his warm golden grin, "Every woman needs a nice home," he said, and went off to hug someone else.

The college also needed new homes. Richard and the RBC board were determined to get rid of the growing trailer court housing staff and married students behind the school. They began a capital campaign to raise funds for a new, two-story staff house of one-and two-bedroom apartments.

A few funds trickled in, but far too slowly. Richard called faculty and staff to a time of prayer and fasting for the needed funds. Sometime later, an anonymous donor called Richard, out of the blue, and offered to pay all the remaining costs for the new apartment building. The donors did not want anyone to know their names, only to honor God by investing in the spiritual formation and education of young adults.

Al Troyer along with Al Yoder supervised the construction of the new campus building.

During our five years in the Rosedale community, we enjoyed the life of the college. I helped write a 40-year history of RBC and worked as a staff writer at RMM. We loved hosting the youth and young adults drawn into our home by our children as they moved into college, began dating, and exploring careers.

For part of our Rosedale years we also provided housing for a woman who claimed to have been part of a Satanic cult and suffered what was diagnosed as Multiple Personality Disorder (MPD) or Dissociative Identity Disorder (DID). Her counselor requested a "safe house" particularly during special seasons like her birthday and Halloween when she was more at risk.

We opened our new home to her. A team of people led by Steve Troyer, also moved in to help provide support and ministry to this troubled woman.

This controversial ministry divided the RBC community, and eventually, in line with counsel from the RBC board of trustees, we asked her to leave our home and distanced ourselves from this "safe house" ministry. I remember the feelings that warred within us—wanting to be available as God's instruments of healing and deliverance to the ill and oppressed—yet not wanting this impulse to overshadow or compromise the ministry of the college.

While working at RBC we also continued our periodic trips to the Turkic world. In the summer of 1993, Open Doors invited us to visit the minority Turkish community in Bulgaria and paid for our expenses. Since the fall of the Iron Curtain, and the opening of Eastern Europe, we'd been hearing about revivals taking place in Bulgaria.

Accompanied by Turkish believers, we made several trips to join what God was doing in the Turkish and Roma/Gypsy communities of Bulgaria. Large groups gathered for worship and street preaching which led to the formation of Turkish congregations. We partnered with a young church in Burgas, thrilled to see their openness and eagerness for fellowship and teaching.

On one occasion we joined a large group who were ministering to a troubled Bulgarian man they had brought in off the street. He wanted healing and deliverance. The group of believers gathered around praying fervently. As they prayed for the troubled young man, he fell to the ground as though dead. They continued praying until suddenly he sprang to his feet loudly praising God in Turkish. The Bulgarian-Turkish ministry team went wild!

"Why is that so unusual?" I asked a woman near me.

"He's Bulgarian!" she yelled. "He doesn't know Turkish, but he's praising God in Turkish tongues, and we can understand what he's saying."

Several years later our son Matt was leading a short-term REACH team to work with this same Bulgarian Turkish community. We began to hear reports that Matt was preaching in Turkish on the streets of Burgas. We'd never heard him preach in English, much less in the Turkish of his childhood.

Open preaching and partnership with Bulgarian Turks after the fall of the Iron Curtain.

Later when we asked Matt what he preached on he said, "Remember when I didn't want to go back to Turkey with you, and Dad cried with me in the back seat on the way to the airport? I told the Bulgarian-Turkish group that, 'All things work together for good.' (Romans 8:28). Even the hard stuff. If I hadn't gone back to Turkey with you that last time, I wouldn't have remembered my Turkish. You have to speak it into adolescence to keep it. That last year really salted it down."

Just when we thought we might be settling into our roles at RBC, helping to equip young adults for Kingdom work, we got a surprising call from Eastern Mennonite Missions. They invited Richard to become the next president of EMM. We loved RBC, but our earlier work and call to serve among the "unreached regions" of the world, made this call especially attractive.

We called stakeholders from LMC/EMM and CMC/RBC to a time of discernment facilitated by our psychiatrist friend Enos Daniel Martin. Both sides shared why they thought we should work with them. As we listened to both sides share their sense of the right next steps for us, we prayed to hear God's voice through it all. A clear but difficult sense of direction emerged. God was calling us to the work at EMM.

We'd only enjoyed four years in our new home. I was just learning about ground cover and mulching for our flower beds. Chad had finished college and moved to Flint, Michigan. Rhoda was engaged to be married, and Matt was at RBC and soon to enter the short-term REACH program.

When I'd left Lancaster to get married in 1968, I never thought I'd come back. There were dozens of Mennonite churches of every stripe in all directions. This was the Mennonite heartland—the place my Wenger and Weaver ancestors had settled back in the 1700s after landing in Philadelphia and travelling west in search of good farmland.

This is where my grandfather A.D. Wenger had led revival meetings and helped to fan the flame of "new birth" and a call to share this good news with the rest of the world. We arrived in Lancaster just as EMM was celebrating 100 years since its founding.

,

These were my people. But so many on a pile? If we were such good "manure," shouldn't we be spread around to bring growth and fruitfulness in other barren places?

Bishop David Thomas, an old friend and member of the LMC/EMM discernment team grinned, held his nose, and wondered if I could choose another metaphor.

We moved to Landisville/Salunga, a short walk from the EMM headquarters in the summer of 1994. My parents had gone to Ethiopia with EMM in 1949 when I was one year old. My dad had worked in EMM's home missions office before leaving to pastor and give time to his grape and flower farmette. I was coming to one of my many physical homes.

Maybe home isn't one place, one people, one tribe? It's many people. God's people. God's call. His place of belonging and service. Himself. His undergirding arms. His whole big Body.

How many different homes had I had? Home defined as a place where you fix meals and change sheets: at least six in Ethiopia, three in Lancaster, Pennsylvania, one in Chesapeake and three college dorms in Harrisonburg, Virginia.

Since marriage Richad and I had lived in Chicago, Illinois, at four homes in Rosedale, Ohio, two in Harrisonburg, Virginia, two in Mechanicsburg and one in Columbus, Ohio, two in Downey, California, three in Goshen, Indiana, three in Turkey, one in north Cyprus, two in Kenya, one in China, one in Salunga, Pennsylvania. In between our many transitions we'd lived for brief seasons with our parents and grandparents.

During the five years in Ohio I spoke at numerous women's meetings and retreats. Most of these women had lived in the same community all their lives. They seemed so comfortable and settled, their furniture lovely and coordinated.

In comparison our life seemed scattered and fragmented, our furnishings eclectic and haphazard. One morning as I prayed about this sense of fragmentation, I suddenly saw in my mind's eye a large colorful patchwork quilt spread out on an elegant, king-size bed.

I'd learned to quilt while in Ohio. Richard had been gifted several quilts after holding renewal meetings in Mennonite churches. We'd received two friendship quilts with blocks lovingly embroidered by friends. Yes, we'd moved a lot, but now we slept under multi-colored patchwork quilts.

"Don't you think blankets are kinda boring?" God whispered to my spirit. "I like quilts!"

The rich colors and textures of our life in the global church have been priceless. And isn't that what I'd wanted most—to dwell in God—with his people—to be part of his universal Body, his Bride? Life was only going to get more colorful.

20

Lancaster, Pennsylvania

Rhoda, Matt, and Chad singing at Richard's EMM Inaugaration.

We moved into a cozy split level at 150 James Street in Landisville, just a short walk from the historic EMM headquarters in Salunga.

The previous owners had filled the front flower bed with bright welcoming pansies. There was a brick patio outback with space for a garden, a front porch shaded by a towering oak. Rhododendron, forsythia, holly, and dogwood sprawled along the sides and back of the house underneath large maple, tulip poplar, and hemlock trees.

The four bedrooms, two and a half baths, and basement gave adequate space to host our children and their families as well as offer hospitality to stateside missionaries, national church leaders, visiting friends, young adults in transition, or others in need.

The first morning after we'd unpacked the moving truck, I stepped to the porch to enjoy the early summer breeze. As I stooped to pull a stray dandelion from the patch of pansies, I heard silvery peals from the carillon of the nearby Lutheran church. "A mighty fortress is our God..." rang out. Hymns played on the hour.

Home in Landisville, PA.

Instantly I remembered the quote from missionary statesman C.T. Studd, *"Some wish to live within the sound of church or chapel bell, but I would build a rescue shop within a yard of hell."*

I knelt crying, a strange mixture of gratitude and burden, on the cement porch. "Oh God. This house, this neighborhood, is so nice, so peaceful. Is this really where you've placed us for this season? Within the sound of chapel bells? How can this home, this work, enable and support others to go where you are not yet known?"

During our first two years the EMM board asked both Richard and me to make initial visits to all EMM locations—or as many as possible—for orientation and assessment. The previous president had left suddenly under the shadow of immoral behavior. We followed the interim leadership of the CFO.

We also helped lead summer retreats for new and returning overseas missionaries as well as stateside church planters, learning to know the EMM team and setting vision and direction for the next season.

Our early overseas travels took us to East Africa—Kenya, Tanzania, Ethiopia, Djibouti, and Uganda. In Latin America we visited Puerto Rico, Haiti, Dominican Republic, Peru, Chile, Venezuela, Honduras, Belize, Guatemala, and El Salvador. In Europe we visited Germany, Albania, Bulgaria, and Wales, in Asia—Hong Kong, Taiwan, China, Indonesia, Singapore, Vietnam, India, the Philippines, Cambodia, and China.

Jewel and Richard walking the Great Wall of China in early days at EMM.

Stateside we visited younger church plants in places like Boston, New York City, New Jersey, New Haven, Philadelphia, Birmingham, Atlanta, and Mobile.

It was an awesome privilege to have this bird's-eye-view of EMM locations around the world. How was God calling us to respond in the current season?

During the Mennonite World Conference in Calcutta, India, in 1997, David Shenk, Global Ministries Director, and Richard, convened a meeting of EMM partners from around the world. The idea of forming an organization called the International Missions Association (IMA) began to emerge with Amor Viviente of Honduras, PIPKA of Indonesia, MKC of Ethiopia, and EMM of North America, joining forces for greater collaboration in mission training and sending.

Certainly missions—"from the west to the rest"—was entering a new phase. A vibrant, short-term program known as Youth Evangelism Service or YES was attracting hundreds of young people who coupled three months of discipleship training with six to nine months of overseas service. Many of the youth who served in YES returned to serve more long-term. Young adults from overseas partner churches also joined YES until the more stringent visa policies implemented after 9/11 in 2001 made this almost impossible.

The work of North American mission teams was becoming increasingly "international." We loved the growing synergy with partner churches. Richard was sometimes reprimanded for spending more time with national church leaders than with the mission teams sent out from North America.

How could EMM partner with the churches in places like Ethiopia and Tanzania—to not only reach the unreached tribes in their countries—but in neighboring countries like Yemen, Sudan, and Somalia where it's much more difficult (and expensive) for western missionaries to serve?

A positive vote by the Bishop Board of Lancaster Mennonite Conference (LMC) and its mission agency, EMM, to join the newly forming Mennonite Church USA as a member conference in 2002 was both preceded and followed by many discussions about new structures and levels of collaboration in North America.

Ever since his young adult years Richard had been asked to serve on committees of the broader Mennonite church—such as the Council on Faith, Life and Strategy and Council on Biblical Interpretation. As this merger moved ahead, he found it deeply unsettling. He knew the broader Mennonite church in ways many in Lancaster did not and believed joining the broader Mennonite church would not be a good fit for the more conservative and evangelically-minded LMC.

The younger EMM-initiated church plants—many including new immigrants—in New England, New Jersey, Philadelphia and the southern cities of Atmore, Mobile, and Birmingham, Alabama, as well as the whole circle of Hispanic churches organized under the Spanish Council, were especially resistant to the idea of a merger with those who may share an historic Swiss German root with LMC but were much less evangelical in their theology.

We asked ourselves what we'd gain by focusing on "family projects and reunions" with the "distant cousins" of the broader Mennonite church more than our own "children" who had come to Christ through EMM church planting efforts up and down the eastern seaboard.

We longed to throw ourselves into the task of "knowing him and making him known," without the endless bureaucratic meetings called to decide how EMM and LMC could and should fit into the broader MC USA structures.

Richard penned the vision, *"As the waters cover the sea,"* and organized EMM to increase focus on the least-reached regions of the world—"mission to world." That's what EMM had done in 1934 when they sent their first overseas workers to Tanzania. Then as new churches emerged the focus shifted to "mission with church" and "church with church." Eventually a healthy, reproducing circle of churches grows to "mission with mission" as the "mission societies" of the partner churches learn from, challenge, and support one another. The IMA is an expression of that "mission with mission" impulse.

***

During our 18 years in Lancaster, the longest we'd ever lived in any one home and region, we planted asparagus, rhubarb, sour cherry and peach trees, and stayed long enough to enjoy the harvest. We walked the country roads by Amish and Mennonite farms near our home.

We were part of three churches, University Christian Fellowship, a new church plant on the campus of Millersville University, Christ the King, a charismatic Mennonite church that had gone through a painful split, and West End Mennonite Fellowship, a new church plant in an old bar in downtown Lancaster.

I took a year of CPE and went to seminary, earning an MTh in Missions from Eastern Baptist (Palmer) Theological Seminary.

We also enjoyed annual retreats with old friends from Ohio and Maryland. On one retreat as we hiked together in the forests of Canaan Valley Resort State Park in West Virginia, we noticed the large number of fallen logs that sank in slow decay into the damp ground.

Then I noticed an old log. Out of the rotting trunk sprang five little evergreens spanning the length of the log.

"What's going on here?" I asked.

"The rotting trunk is the most fertile spot on the forest floor," the guide explained. "We call the old decaying logs 'tree nurseries.' Out of the old log's death comes a whole crop of little new trees."

Tears sprang to my eyes. "Jesus, remember when I tried so hard to try to fit in—in Lancaster, Goshen, Rosedale? Submitting to those community expectations? Remember when I thought you were sending us to Hong Kong and I chaffed under my husband's indecision?

Oh, and those difficult days living out of suitcases in Kenya, learning language and then our premature expulsion from Turkey?"

I straddled the dying log between two little trees—enjoying the new life bursting from the fallen giant.

***

Richard had two major health crises during this season of work at EMM, a heart attack followed by open heart surgery in 1999 and mesenteric bypass surgery in 2007. Both of these major life-threatening surgeries had their roots in the intense abdominal radiation he was given following his bout with testicular cancer in 1975. It is now known that radiation causes thickening of the arteries. As a result of that treatment, his renal arteries had thickened, driving blood pressure up to dangerous levels.

This led to the near-fatal heart attack on Sandbridge Beach in Virginia, at a Wenger family reunion. Richard collapsed suddenly in the midst of a beach football game. I rushed to his side as his eyes rolled back. Nephew Joe Shenk ran to call 911. I frantically thumped Richard's chest, trying to remember my long-ago CPR training. He slowly came to, opened his eyes, and sat up. A doctor told me later the thumps likely saved his life—jump-starting his heart.

The squad arrived and examined Richard, wanting to take him to the hospital, but since he now seemed fine, except for high blood pressure, he brushed it off. The head EMT pulled me aside and made me promise I'd take him in. "People don't pass out for no reason," he said.

All the way back to the house where we changed out of swimwear and showered, Richard tried to persuade me not to take him to the hospital. He didn't succeed. After a long wait in the ER, they finally heard our story and took him in for testing. The doctor flung back the curtain and stood at the end of the bed, clipboard in hand. "Sorry to ruin your vacation, but you've just had a heart attack. We're admitting you to the cardiac unit for further testing and treatment."

After this major open-heart bypass surgery, we paused, took more time for country walks, to identify trees and flowers. But we quickly plunged back into the work we loved. We never quite refrained from discussing work during vacation days or "sabbaths" as Human Resources personnel urged. Our work was so stimulating and enjoyable that it often felt almost like "sabbath."

After the heart attack a friend asked Richard how he felt about the near-death experience. He said that he felt no anxiety, that he sometimes is surprised that he's lived as long as he has. He used to think that perhaps he'd die as a martyr at a much younger age. Now or 30 years ago? What's the difference?

He lived life with a peaceful, positive outlook. Once when we were leading an RBC study term in Ethiopia, a student commented that he'd never heard Richard say anything negative or judgmental about anyone. He'd been teaching *History of Missions* for the past three weeks as we visited various regions of the country. Then as sort of a test case someone suggested, "Why don't we ask Richard how he feels about the devil?"

The student sidled up the aisle of the swaying bus to Richard's seat. "Hey, Richard, I've got a deep theological question for you. What do you think about the devil?"

Richard looked at the student with his wonderful warm smile. The flickering sunlight filtering through the grove of acacia trees highlighted his hazel eyes. "Well," he replied, "I'd say he's pretty good at what he does, wouldn't you?"

During our last years at EMM I picked up administration for programs in the Middle East, grateful to see that region expanding with work in Jordan, Israel, Lebanon, Egypt, Morocco, and Turkey. I also continued writing stories of God at work around the world. Most were published in the *Missionary Messenger* and the *Mennonite Weekly Review.*

I also spoke at dozens of "Young Moms" gatherings from York to Weaverland—telling stories of God's work around the world. Once after speaking about a visit to our daughter's family in China and showing a slide of her holding their one-year-old son, a woman came up to talk.

"Did I understand you to say that the cute little boy on that one slide is your grandson?" she said.

"Yes, they've been there for about a dozen years," I answered.

Daughter Rhoda with young son Jadon.

"You must be a much better Christian than I am," she said, shaking her head. "I could never let my grandchildren go that far away. We get together every Sunday afternoon."

On another occasion as I shared my spiritual pilgrimage at World Missions Institute, a pre-field training and orientation for missionaries, I told stories from my boarding school days—the pain of family separations and my struggles to forgive Mrs. Wallace.

As Richard and I processed my sharing at WMI, he said, "I wonder if your forgiveness for Mrs. Wallace needs to go a little deeper."

Instantly I knew he was right. I enjoyed too much making her look like a monster, getting laughs and sympathy at her expense. Then a surprising email came from the Sudan Interior Mission (SIM), the mission organization that administered Bingham Academy. They had received unfavorable reports from "adult survivors" of the school and were reaching out to all former students for reports of mistreatment and abuse. They offered counseling and space to share and process with others.

I wrote to share some of my most painful experiences, but also said I was working to forgive Mrs. Wallace and now even wished I could talk to her woman-to-woman—to hear her story and learn more about the pain, fear, and disappointments that drove her to act as she did. Could SIM supply contact information?

My SIM correspondent wrote back to say that sadly, Mrs. Wallace had died of cancer, but Mr. Wallace was living and had recently written a book on Mrs. Wallace's life. "You probably don't want to hear this," my SIM correspondent wrote. "But it's called *The Shaping of a Saint.*"

Oh my. I immediately ordered a copy and emailed Mr. Wallace. He'd taught me grades 5-7 and was an excellent teacher. I'm sure he never knew how I hated his wife. His book was a loosely edited version of Mrs. Wallace's letters home to her family in Canada. She had suffered too, looking after other missionaries' children when she had thought she was going to be a "real" missionary on the "front lines." She was a real person who loved and lost.

I was able to lay Mrs. Wallace to rest.

***

As the members and activities of the IMA began to grow, Mennonite World Conference also began work to form a Global Missions

Fellowship (GMF). The first meeting was held in Almaty, Kazakhstan, in 2008.

During our years in Turkey, we'd known the "Turkic World" spanned from the Uighur peoples of western China to the Bulgarian Turks of Europe. But during our years in Turkey, the Central Asian republics of Tajikistan, Turkmenistan, Uzbekistan, Kyrgyzstan, Kazakhstan, and Azerbajan were all part of the USSR and not open to western visitors.

At the GMF meetings we met young Turkic pastors who said they thought they'd always been Muslim, before realizing that there were significant pockets of Christian faith in their tribes before the advent of Islam and Marxism. One historian noted, "We first had Christian roots. Now the old stump is pushing up new shoots."

We reveled in the indigenous music spilling from a variety of unique stringed instruments. As we observed the joyous worship, head-scarved women pulled us to our feet to join the dance. One took my hand and thrust her ornate silver ring on my finger. Nothing has ever made me feel more like I'm part of the international Bride of Christ.

As we sat around a long low table on the floor of a festive yurt to partake of a feast in our honor, the Kazakh chief placed a platter holding the head of the slaughtered sheep in front of our leader. He explained that they had an ancient custom of scoring the head of the sheep with a cross before serving it. They never knew why they did this. They just thought it was an X. But now that they are Christians, they realize it's a symbol of Jesus Christ, the Lamb of God, who takes away the sins of the world with his sacrifice on the cross.

After returning to Lancaster, Richard was scheduled to speak one Sunday in one of the more than 200 congregations that comprised LMC at the time. As we entered the church Richard was whisked away to join the leadership team for their pre-service prayer time. I stood alone in the back of the church, not recognizing anyone.

I noticed two young women engaged in deep conversation, children running around. Everyone looked like they felt at home, like they belonged. I was an outsider. No one knew me. I'll never fit in anywhere, I muttered to myself. Strangeness washed over me. And a hunger-to-belong. How could I feel more at home in exotic Kazakhstan than in Lancaster?

"Jewel, you do belong. I am here. Remember? I am your dwelling place," the Spirit whispered.

"Of course! Bitter, narcissistic self-pity be gone!" Then I noticed a woman standing all by herself. I hurried over to get acquainted and draw her into the circle of belonging.

In 2011 as Richard reached retirement age, he began to feel that it was time to bring closure to his service at EMM. After five years as president of RBC and now nearly 18 as president of EMM he wearied of the burdens of being a CEO—setting direction, staffing, balancing budgets. We also sensed we wanted to move back to Ohio to be nearer to our children and grandchildren. Or should we go back overseas ourselves, maybe to China where our daughter and her family had been living?

We spent weeks sorting and packing. Downsizing. A lot of old and new books. A big box of plaques, awards, trophies. We were moving to a small apartment.

"I don't want to pay to haul all these books to Ohio, but I need to say goodbye," Richard said.

He brushed off the dust and sat down among his beloved books. Many went to libraries and used book auctions. Then I took that box of trophies and awards off to the dumpster. Am I really doing this? Dumping out all the memorabilia? One large, well-sculpted wooden trophy was especially hard to part with, but as we had sorted things, it fell over and broke. Now it teetered on the edge of the large green dumpster.

In that moment the old hymn I'd sung in childhood, back in southern Virginia peach country, rushed into my mind, *"So I'll cherish the old rugged cross, Till my trophies at last I lay down; I will cling to the old rugged cross, And exchange it someday for a crown."*

"Till my trophies at last I lay down..." Richard drove in with a U-Haul truck and there splashed on the side of the U-Haul in bold colorful detail was the picture of two red pandas feeding in a bamboo forest. Red pandas are unique to China.

21

Global South Partnerships

On a summer break during our two years in China we managed to find panda tee shirts for all the grandchildren.

Ever since I was a little girl, I'd wanted to be a missionary to China. I'd enjoyed the writings of authors like Isobel Kuhn and Pearl Buck. I'd cried over the missionary stories of people like John and Betty Stamm who'd been killed in the Boxer Rebellion. During our years at EMM we'd visited university English teachers placed by Mennonite Partners in China (MPC).

Our daughter and her husband were now serving on a mission team in China and needed to relocate from their high altitude setting to Chengdu because of the birth of their third child. They invited us to consider joining their team for two years. Our retirement from EMM made this possible.

I applied to MPC for a job teaching conversational English to graduate students at Sichuan Normal University in Chengdu.

I had to leave early for orientation, but Richard stayed a month longer to assist with childcare during the birth of Chad and Deborah's Jamie Richard, July 30, and Matt and Colleen's Kenna Dove, July 31, 2012.

In China we lived with our daughter and her family spending many happy hours joining their household activities. While I commuted by bus to teach conversational English to Chinese graduate students, Richard volunteered to teach English in our grandson's nearby elementary school. He also taught stints at Bethany International University in Singapore, in an underground Chinese missionary training school in Shanghai, at a Bible school in Indonesia, leadership and mission training in Ethiopia, Tanzania, and Kenya.

Our daughter's fourth child was born during our two years in China. We spent summers in the U.S. assisting with childcare during two weeks of Choral Camp at RBC when various of our children and grandchildren were involved with the camps.

After the two years in China, we set up life in the RBC duplex beside Matt and Colleen and their five children. This arrangement helped facilitate a more itinerant lifestyle that allowed us to invest large blocks of time walking with international partners.

As we prayed about sources of income for this next season, it seemed we had sufficient funds to cover basic living expenses, but not costly international travel. We could have worked to raise funds from interested friends and churches for these extra expenses. But we hoped we wouldn't have to go that route.

"Out of the blue" we got a call from an old friend who flies for United Airlines. We'd not heard from him for years. He explained that he had a "buddy pass" he could give to anyone. He'd been thinking and praying about who to give it to, and Richard's name came to mind as someone who travels a lot.

We gratefully accepted the "buddy pass" which saved us thousands of dollars in air travel although the "standby" method occasionally left Richard stranded in airports near and far.

When we shared a Missions Day sermon at the annual meeting of the Conservative Mennonite Conference (now Rosedale Network of Churches), Richard mentioned, in passing, that our 1997 Honda Accord with its nearly 500,000 miles, was too old to be allowed on the streets of Singapore.

Afterwards, a businessman came up to him and shared that he was feeling led to give us a minivan that would be allowed on the streets of Singapore! This beautiful and timely gift enabled us to enjoy great times hauling grandchildren, as well as comfortable travel on longer trips.

We spent several months at a time in Turkey assisting with a church plant that was being led by the widow of one of the early Gaziantep believers. We spent three months based at Amani Gardens in Nairobi, Kenya, while visiting, preaching, and teaching down country in Kenya, Uganda, and Tanzania. We walked with a circle of Bengali churches and church planters based in Siliguri, India. We lived at Meserete Kristos College in Ethiopia and assisted with various trainings and seminars.

On a visit to western Uganda to visit a circle of churches planted by the Kenya Mennonite Church we stayed in the home of a local leader who lived on a banana plantation. He welcomed us warmly, and gave us a tour of his banana plantation, explaining the types for juicing, roasting, mashing, frying, and eating fresh. I had no idea there were so many kinds of bananas.

Then he looked at us and said, "This is your plantation. Please feel free to come back anytime. You're always welcome to stay with us."

In a flash I remembered the tearful separations from my parents, my children, my husband, the many and varied homes we'd lived in. I remembered that Jesus promised his followers many more homes and relationships when they left their beloved peoples and possessions for his sake.

"Thanks, God," I smiled. "Now I even own a banana plantation!"

Also during this season my parents began to need more round-the-clock assistance, so we began spending time in Lancaster to assist with this need. Richard taught Introduction to Missions at RBC. We helped lead an RBC cross-cultural term to Ethiopia.

Invitations came from near and far. In the fall of 2018, we planned a special fiftieth anniversary camping trip in the lovely van we'd been gifted. The trip took us through the U.S. and Canadian Rockies, Yosemite and the Pacific Northwest. We interrupted the camping to teach in Singapore for a week and attend an IMA meeting in Mexico.

Richard and Jewel celebrating 50 years of their life together.

Last IMA meeting Richard attended in Huatabampo, Mexico.

In between teaching and ministry trips Richard worked on a book, *Footsteps of Jesus,* that traced the spread of the gospel from the early church to the present. He'd been using much of this material in the teaching he was doing around the world. He reveled in the joy of seeing and participating in the expansion of the church in his generation. To see Turks sharing the gospel with Turks, Bengalis sharing the gospel with Bengalis, Ugandans with Ugandans...or Hondurans sharing with Mexicans, Ethiopians with Somalis...

I was in Lancaster helping with care for my father in June of 2019 when Richard arrived home from a teaching stint in Medan, Indonesia. He was complaining of abdominal discomfort which we thought might be parasites and headed to a local doctor for tests.

He called from the hospital where the doctor had sent him for more conclusive imaging. "The doctor has discovered the cause of my discomfort," he said.

"Oh, good," I said. Glad to finally have some answers. "What is it?"

"It's late," he said. "I'll tell you when I get home."

We were staying in the basement of the home that had become my youngest brother Tom and his wife Keiko's. Dad Wenger was still living there, but there were plans for him to move, and remodeling had begun.

When Richard arrived, we sat together in the basement family room at 2186 Old Philadelphia Pike, the home where we'd become engaged for marriage, the family home I'd left from when we married in 1968.

He took my hands in his. "The doctor said the tests show that I have pancreatic cancer. He advises that we go home to Ohio immediately and begin exploring treatment options there."

The grief and shock of that news hit like a sledgehammer. Our eyes filled with tears as the reality of the news sank in. "Really? He's sure?" I queried, grasping for shreds of hope.

"Yes, it's obvious from the imaging," he said. We hugged for a long time, then lay beside each other on the floor mattress—each frozen in our own thoughts and griefs. The unknowns of the next months swirled around us like dense fog.

After our long drive to Ohio through early summer sunshine I lay in bed filled with the draining exhaustion of grief. I'd never suffered from depression, but suddenly I understood those who do. If only I could sleep away the reality that was bursting upon us. But I couldn't.

Emails and phone calls shared the sad news with our family and friends. Our daughter Rhoda and her husband Keith Miller and their four sons made plans to spend the summer in the U.S. but needed to return for work and school in Asia in the fall.

We spent the next months in doctor's appointments and visiting alternative health clinics, always in consultation with our children. Doctors held out tiny bits of hope for a regimen of severe chemo that would shrink the pancreatic tumor followed by radical Whipple surgery. We started down that route.

After about only a week of treatment Richard looked at me pleadingly over the lunch table, asking if he could be released from the mind-numbing chemo. It had already taken him to the edge of despair. Discontinuing chemo was giving up on the only shred of hope for a cure offered by the medical community. He felt like the "walking dead," like he was descending into hell. He was doing it for me—for our family—although it wasn't his choice. He wanted to live life fully and completely as long as the Lord gave him life and breath.

I hated to see the way he was so diminished, here and yet not here. I paraphrased an old poem, "These things do I despise, chemotherapy and lies and anything at all that dims the light in Richard's eyes."

"It's okay with me," I said. Our eyes met, glued with liquid love. Then he grabbed me in a tight embrace as shuddering sobs shook our bodies.

We gathered to sing, pray, and share memories as Richard's life on earth faded away.

In the next months we tried a variety of fresh juices and supplements recommended by alternative practitioners. We took long walks most days. We spent rich times with children and grandchildren as well as other friends from near and far who came with stories, memories, and words of appreciation. We were part of a small group at MCF. Richard also visited men in the Tri-County Jail in Mechanicsburg, and we offered short-term lodging to a man upon his release.

I've sometimes wished he had written more down—like his well-known sermon on the two trees in the Garden of Eden, preached in North and South America, Asia, Africa, and Europe. It's been translated into Spanish, Amharic, Swahili, Bengali, Indonesian, Chinese, Turkish...He'd urge his listeners to choose "life" not mere "right"—the Tree of Life as opposed to the Tree of the Knowledge of Good and

Evil. And in the last weeks of his life, choosing "life" meant sitting with broken and angry man in the county jail.

On December 7, just eight days before his death, he played the role of Simeon in our church's live nativity. I was Anna. Just like Simeon of old whose eyes had seen the baby Jesus—the glory of the Lord in the temple—Richard was ready to depart in peace.

On December 11 he became confused and began repeating himself. A visit to the hospital confirmed that he was "actively dying." We brought him home, setting up a hospice bed in the living room.

For several days we gathered around his bed and easy chair, singing and telling stories. We fed him bowls of his favorite raspberry-chocolate chunk ice-cream from Graeters. Several of his siblings came to share words of appreciation and farewell. Our daughter and family were still on their way home from Asia and called to say goodbye.

On the morning of December 14 Richard asked me to open his laptop. He couldn't type anymore but tried dictating words to meet the deadline for his last *Mennonite Weekly Review* column. The swift capable fingers that had typed letters, reports, memos, books, articles, and sermons lay still. I suggested several concluding sentences to wrap up the column he'd already begun. He sighed in resignation. It was painful to see his brilliant mind labor and stumble over words he still wanted to share.

All I could think was, "Rage, rage against the dying of the light."

One week before Richard's death we played the roles of Simeon and Anna in our church's Christmas pageant.

That afternoon and evening our immediate family continued to talk, sing, and pray around his bed. Toward evening he slipped into a coma and then shortly before midnight slowly stopped his labored breathing. Seventy-four years of abundant life on earth had come to an end. He entered into Life.

I was bereft, cloven in two. For 51 years I'd forged a partnership with this beloved man, "two becoming one" for the Kingdom. We argued, laughed, hiked, prayed. Faced God and the world. Together. Though often separated physically, we were best friends. His children and grandchildren loved him. Many guests at the funeral said, "He was like a father to me."

He truly had many "children." But only one wife, and he loved her well.

In the hospital when I finally realized that death was ripping us apart, a deep and primal wail burst from my lips. The nurses came running. "Do you need a chaplain?"

"No, thank you," I said. "I already have two." I grasped Richard's arm and that of my son.

We chose to chisel Habakkuk 2:14 on Richard's tombstone. "And the earth shall be filled with the knowledge of the glory of the Lord, as the waters cover the sea!" We have caught glimpses of that glory. It continues to spread around the world.

22

Epilogue

Christmas 2024: our Showalter family Christmas five years after Richard's death.

Sometimes I think of my life as a series of "altars"—places where I've seen the face of God, heard his still, small voice. In this memoir I've shared the most significant of these "altars" that have truly altered my life. I've often felt like Elizabeth Barrett Browning that "every bush is aflame with the fire of God, but only those who see take off their shoes..." Or like Jacob rising from his stony pillow with angels in his eyes, "surely God is in this place, but I was unaware of it." He built a Bethel altar. It is my prayer that you too will see the light of God in every bush, every face, every experience—that you will pause, take off your shoes, and be changed.

***

In January 2002 I had the privilege of attending the 50th anniversary celebrations of the founding of the Meserete Kristos Church in Addis Ababa, Ethiopia.

I looked out on a huge sea of brown faces. The Misrak Cathedral could hold 5,000, but there were 8-10,000 on the grounds, filling the food tent and browsing through displays.

Choirs in brilliant robes of maroon, green, and yellow swayed and sang in haunting Amharic melodies. I could catch a few Amharic words. God. Lord. Praise. Worship. The lilting "joy cry" crescendoed then faded to a murmur, rising and falling like waves on a beach.

The church had grown to 100,000 since those first secretive baptisms 50 years ago, and in 2025 there are more than a million who assemble for worship in MKC churches.

But at that glorious 50th anniversary celebration I suddenly remembered 47 years earlier when I'd lain in my crib shivering violently with yet another attack of malaria. Then a moment later I was burning hot. Too hot for any blankets. I flung back the covers and stripped to my underwear. I stood up weakly and grasping the wooden crib side cried for a drink.

Four years later I remembered pressing my nose against the cold window of the green VW van. We were pulling out the lane of the

HMMM Hospital compound in Nazareth heading back to boarding school in Addis Ababa. I strained through the dust swirling up in our wake to catch one last glimpse of home, of Mama and Papa waving from beside the brilliant bougainvillea that vined over our doorway. Tears blinded my eyes. I didn't want to leave home.

During summer breaks, I remembered sitting with other Ethiopian children under the big flat-topped acacia tree on the hospital compound. We sang, "Yesus in da wadadun,"—Jesus Loves Me, This I Know, and "Yeah semay birhan"—Heavenly Sunshine. We joined a small group of adults on backless wooden benches for an Amharic sermon in one of the hospital buildings. We knelt on the hard cement floor and prayed the Lord's Prayer.

That was most of what I remembered of the Ethiopian church of my childhood. But here at the 50th anniversary of the first baptisms we were witnessing the joy, the appreciation for what the early missionaries had taught and modeled. We were seeing vibrant, brand-new expressions of a deeply rooted and expanding Ethiopian faith.

Suddenly my childhood bouts of malaria, the lonely years in boarding school didn't seem as bad. Or rather they still seemed bad, but the muted bad of labor pains—almost forgotten for the joy of kissing the tiny cheeks of a perfect baby, or the pain of a grueling workout—eclipsed by the joy of sprinting across the finish line—first.

After a life spent in national and international teaching, church planting, administration, writing, and accompaniment, Jewel Showalter lives in the small country town of Rosedale, Ohio. She loves sharing life and telling stories with the Rosedale Bible College community, her home church, Forty One (formerly Mechanicsburg Christian Fellowship) and her energetic family of three married children and 14 grandchildren.

Appendices

Appendix A: The Church at Sea: 1952-1969

(A biographical sketch from the lives of Lloyd and Sara (Oberholtzer) Weaver, my maternal grandparents.)

When M. Lloyd Weaver stepped off the bobbing launch onto the Jacob's rope ladder swinging precariously from the side of the large Japanese ocean liner, he knew he had to go up. The launch pulled away as he climbed the ladder. Down was only the deep green water of the Norfolk, Va., harbor; up – a shipload of foreigners who needed the gospel. And this is what urged him aboard. He had only one Japanese-English New Testament stuffed in his coat and almost lost that on the treacherous climb. But he clambered aboard and immediately began making friends.

Only five short years earlier Lloyd and Sara Weaver had owned a thriving delicatessen business in Lancaster, Pa. As the crowds of people thronged about the market stand buying the quality smoked meats and cheeses Sara remembers thinking, "We're feeding these people physically. When can we make it our business to feed people spiritually?"

Although they were already grandparents and in their upper forties, they both felt that they should sell their business and go into full-time evangelistic work. Lloyd was already taking off one day a week to give to Jewish evangelism in Philadelphia, but this wasn't enough. No specific call had come from the church, but they moved ahead on faith and decided to sell their business.

Shortly after that decision Harold Eshleman, chair of the Jewish evangelism committee for Virginia Mennonite Conference, had meetings in the area and asked to see the Weavers. He invited them to consider beginning Jewish evangelistic work in Newport News, Va.

Lancaster Mennonite Conference also asked them to work among Jews in Philadelphia, but after praying for guidance the Weavers said they knew without question that God was calling them to Newport News.

Weavers moved to Newport News, Virginia, in 1948, and began visiting Jewish homes and businesses making many friends in the neighborhood. They named their large, two-story white frame home on 52nd St, House of Peace.

When their contacts led two young Jewish boys to conversion and baptism into the Christian church the once-friendly Jewish community suddenly became hostile.

"You've gone too far," Lloyd was warned. "Don't be too surprised if a brick comes crashing through your window."

Although the Weavers tried to keep Jewish contacts open, the door appeared to be closing. Then one day when Lloyd stopped for coffee in a bar, a new door for ministry began to open. He was chatting with the Arab bar tender when he noticed a young Chinese man sipping a Coke on the other side of the bar. "Suddenly, like a bolt out of the clear blue sky, I heard God say, 'Go back and talk to that boy,'" Lloyd said.

Amid the barroom clamor Lloyd hurried back to where 24-year-old S.C. Ten sat. He had been left behind by his Chinese ocean liner to recover from appendicitis. He could speak no English and the Weavers knew no Chinese, but Lloyd knew no strangers. During the seven weeks until Ten's ship returned, Lloyd brought him home every day for a meal. Together they prayed, learned English, and Ten began reading the Christian Chinese literature the Weavers bought for him.

When Ten's ship, the S.S. Hassan, returned, he rejoined the crew, and to his delight, discovered a Christian shipmate. They studied the Bible together, and when the ship returned to Newport News Ten requested baptism and became the first member of the far-flung Church at Sea.

Sara remembers the scene of Ten's baptism. After the service he walked around their living room beaming and patting his chest. "Me so happy. Me so happy," he exclaimed in broken English.

Although their first opening for what grew into a unique 20-year ministry among oriental seamen, was with an ordinary sailor, the Weavers learned the importance of contacting the captain and officers of the crew, such as the first mate, the doctor, chief radio operator, and the purser. There men were educated, understood English, and were able to influence the other sailors under them.

The Weavers literally learned "the ropes." Lloyd checked with agents and newspapers to learn of the oriental ships' arrival times. An average of 8-10 ships a week entered the ports of Newport News and Norfolk. There were some Chinese and Korean ships, but predominately Japanese ships came to load up on coal to aid in the rebuilding of their war-torn country.

The oriental seamen filled the cities as their ships waited, sometimes as long as a week, for a berth in the coal pier. The Weavers' eyes were opened to the needs of the lonely sailors and the House of Peace became a haven. Lloyd would fill his car with officers and bring them home for one of Sara's refreshing meals. She also picked up ideas from their guests and was soon serving new dishes like fried rice and sukiyaki.

Together the Weavers and the seamen learned to play American games, shop or picnic in the country. There were friendly Japanese-American softball games. On one occasion Lloyd helped a captain purchase a washing machine to take back home and arranged for a truck to deliver the purchase. The captain was amazed that Lloyd, a minister, was humble enough to do such a lowly job.

The seamen were always intrigued by the sign House of Peace which greeted them from the porch as they entered. This formed a vivid contrast to the American destruction of Nagasaki and Hiroshima. These Mennonites were different from other Americans they had known.

As the ministry grew Lloyd no longer had to swing alone up the fragile-looking rope ladders. Now he was usually greeted by friends from former visits or sailors who had heard about the "tsoumi man" (the one who teaches against sin).

Even though the ship's steps slanting up the side were better than a rope ladder they still weren't very steady. And if the ship was standing empty, the end of the hanging stairway was high about the pier. Occasionally Lloyd had to hoist Sara ahead of him and then pull himself up the 3-4 foot span. Rain and snow also made the steps treacherous. Once safely on board the Weavers led Bible studies in the ship's salon for a crowd of 10-25 men.

Sometimes they'd show slides Lloyd had taken in the Holy Land and tell the story of the Hebrew people and the Messiah. The men always enjoyed Sara's flannelgraph lessons on the creation and other Bible stories as the pictures made the stories easier to understand.

"They liked to hear a woman teach," Lloyd explained. "It's an unusual thing in their culture." Sara also spoke more slowly than Lloyd, who in his friendly enthusiasm kept up a constant stream of questions and explanations. Often the captain interpreted for the rest of the crew. Sometimes friends and other church members accompanied the Weavers on board and shared in singing and witness. Sometimes the crew treated the guests with a delicious oriental meal.

But not all the captains were friendly. Lloyd chuckled as he remembered one "little old hard Japanese" who tried to keep them from coming aboard. But Lloyd had other friends among the crew who said the captain had no right to forbid their friends from visiting. Interestingly, this particular ship was dry-docked several weeks for repairs after a gas explosion caused by wet coal. The Weavers persisted in visiting the ship and Sara even baked a cake for the captain. Although he was a Buddhist, he warmed up enough to accept a New Testament before he left. Buddhism was the dominant religion held by the older seamen. There was also some Shintoism, but most of the younger men professed no faith.

C.C. Wu, a Chinese university graduate who spoke perfect English, looked up the Weavers at their home before they had time to visit his ship. He had been so impressed by the change he saw in the life of S.C. Ten, an ordinary sailor and the first member of the Church at Sea he came to ask the Weavers what had caused the change in Ten's life. Wu came for further teaching every time the ship returned and eventually, he also became a Christian.

After Wu's conversion he began praying for the release of his wife and their seven-year-old son, whom he had never met because of the rules of mainland China. God miraculously granted his request and Wu became an outstanding evangelist among his own people. When his ship docked at ports along the way, he'd look up Chinese names in that city's telephone directories and send post cards with gospel messages printed in Chinese.

Later the captain of the S.S. Hassan, Y.C. Lou also became a Christian. Thirteen years after his conversion he told the Weavers how God had guided him in the rescue of two shipwrecked Indian sailors in the middle of the Pacific Ocean. One night as his ship sped along in the darkness he thought he heard a cry. But after turning and searching most of the night the crew became discouraged and gave up in disbelief. Lou idled the ship the rest of the night as he prayed and in the morning he spotted a white speck through his binoculars. The two men who had been clinging to a board for three days cried like babies when they were lifted aboard.

By 1960 after distributing hundreds of New Testaments, Bible story books, scripture text calendars and tracts, Lloyd was told by one friend, Captain Nakajima, who had not yet become a Christian, "Do you know that you are a very famous man on our ships? Our ships all know about you."

Lloyd and Sara were surprised by their fame. "It's not us," they said. "It's the gospel that's famous!" And they continued telling stories, fixing meals, and playing golf -- "For the sake of the Gospel" – their motto.

Not only did they enjoy sharing the gospel with sailors who had never heard before, their ministry encouraged the few believers who were occasionally on board. One, a Japanese Christian, Dr. Orishima, told them that after meeting them he was instrumental in helping a poor unhappy sailor who jumped overboard. The captain put the doctor in charge of the near-dead sailor when he was rescued and the "medicine" the doctor gave was a bilingual New Testament given him by the Weavers. Dr. Orishima wrote, "Shibata read very earnestly the New Testament, and I taught him every day and night about Christ. This made him change his mind, and in his mind grew up the hope and pleasure for life. From his face darkness and agony disappeared and a smile of hope took place..."

The Weavers built a lasting friendship with Korean Youngsoo Chun who had been flown in to serve as engineer on a reconditioned ship given to Korea by the United States. Before he left he become a Christian and wrote faithfully to ask for their advice. When he met a young woman who worked at a Mennonite orphanage in Tague he asked their permission to marry. After marriage his wife wrote the Weavers, "How could my husband ever have become a Christian if he hadn't gone to Newport News?" He and his family now live in Seoul, and have maintained contact with Weavers' children and grandchildren.

One of the greatest thrills of their 20-year ministry was when three Buddhists knelt in the Weaver living room for baptism. The little Church at Sea grew to 25 members in all parts of the globe, touching back at Newport News for encouragement and refreshment whenever possible. Lloyd estimates that another time as many seamen were also saved through their ministry but joined churches in their homelands.

One seaman friend expressed it this way, "Mr. and Mrs. Weaver, there are little flowers blooming all over the world in places where you have never been because you sowed seeds in Newport News." Captain S. Yajima put it like this, "Mr. Weaver is heaven's most diligent agent for my Japanese people."

Several times customs men suspected Lloyd of being a narcotics agent, rather than an agent of heaven, but even they soon learned that he was really and truly "the Bible man," and they couldn't risk an encounter without receiving a Bible and an invitation to salvation. The trunk they suspected contained only Bibles and Christian literature.

During their 20-year outreach to oriental seamen the Weavers distributed 6,629 New Testaments, mostly bilingual. They found the seamen hungry for reading material. "Whoever listened to our message received a New Testament," Lloyd said, and many a sailor went away bowing, both hands clasping the precious book.

A Japanese lady doctor whom the Weavers nicknamed "the Queen of Sheba" heard of them in Japan and came on a voyage expressly to meet them. The ship docked in Newport News, and she waited on board all day so as not to miss their visit. Lloyd happened to be visiting ships in Norfolk that day, but when he returned he had the strange feeling that he should stop at the Newport News harbor to see if any ships had come in. He soon came home bringing "the Queen" and an interpreter. She asked questions and made notations with pencil and paper. They gave her a New Testament, but have never heard from her again.

Newport News and Norfolk form one of the world's largest harbors, and at the time Weavers began this unique outreach, as many as 75 ships from all over the world visited weekly. The Weavers retired to Harrisonburg, Va., in 1969. Around that time newly built, modern coal and cargo piers were shifting the bulk of the shipping business away from their old home, the House of Peace, in Newport News.

"Only eternity will reveal the good that was done in our ministry," Sara noted.

Appendix B: Biblical Nursery Rhymes

Hush l'l Baby

Hush l'l baby, don't cry a tear.
Mother and Daddy love you dear.
When little dear you cry and fret,
Mother and Daddy love you yet.
When you've got a belly ache
Daddy'll give you a kindly shake
When your belly ache goes away
Mommy'll give you a rattle to play
When that little pink rattle gets broke
Daddy'll put you in the tub to soak.
When your water drains down the sink
Mommy'll give you some milk to drink.
When your milk spills away on the floor
Daddy will surely get you more.
Always know whate'er befall
God the Father loves you best of all
He's the God of old and young.
Praise to the Father three in one
Let's sing praises every day
Ha-la-la-la-la-lu-le-ay

Daniel

Daniel was a brave man
Daniel took a stand
Daniel prayed to his God in a foreign land

Men came to Daniel's house
Daniel was at prayer
Men took him to the king and gave him quite a scare.

Threw Daniel in the den
Lions waited there
Would you dare to say a prayer if lions waited there?

God shut the lions' mouths
God shut them tight
Mad roaring lions couldn't even take a bite!

Good Morning

Good morning to my daughter
Good morning to my sons
God's made another day for you
To run and have your fun.
He loves to see you run and play
Each glad and happy day
And listens well and carefully
To everything you say

Samson

Samson, Samson, lion killer
Had a wife and couldn't still her
She put him in a prison cell
And there she kept him very well
Shaved him hair
Reduced his fare
Until he felled the temple pillar

Baa, Baa Lost Sheep

Baa, baa, lost sheep
Have you gone astray?
Yes, sir, yes, sir, lost my way,
Once in the brambles
Once in the leaves
And once on a hill all covered with trees.

Baa, baa lost sheep
Are you really found?
Yes sir, yes, sir, homeward bound.
Snatched from the brambles
Brushed from the leaves
Rescued on a hill all covered with trees.

Prophet Samuel

Prophet Samuel
Bring your horn.
A king is waiting
To be sworn.

Where's the king
Who waits the horn?
Hiding in baggage
All forlorn

Peter

Crow, cock, crow
Cock crow thrice
One he stammered
Two he stuttered
Three he cursed and swore
Sad, bad Peter
Denied his Lord no more.

Zachee

Wee little Zachee
Climbed up a tree
Up a wall, up a tree
Anything to see
Straining to see Jesus
Sighting o'er the throng
Is that Jesus under me?
I know that I've done wrong!
Wee little Zachee
Climbed down a tree
Down a wall, down a tree
Anything to be
Sitting with the Master
Searching for the way
"If I've cheated any man
Four times I will repay."

Mary, Mary, Virgin Mary

Mary, Mary, Virgin Mary
How does your Jesus grow?
With stature tall
And love for all
God's people here below.

Twelve baskets

Twelve baskets bare
Twelve baskets full
Twelve baskets heaped with food
For everyone to share

Jesus saw them bare
Jesus made them full
Jesus made them heaped with food
For everyone to share

We saw them bare
We saw them full
We saw them headed with food
For everyone to share

Sling the stone

Sling the stone
Sling the stone
Sling the small rock
Here a giant
So defiant
Listen to him mock!

Praise the Lord
Praise the Lord
The small stone round
Sent the giant
So defiant
Toppling to the ground

John the Baptist

John, John Baptist
Whither is your lair?
Eating locusts
Sipping honey
Dressed in camel's hair

John, John Baptist
Wherefore do you teach?
Baptizing crowds
Preparing hearts
"Salvation is for each!"

Jacob and Esau

Jacob and Esau his brother fell out
And what do you think it was all about?
Isaac loved Esau, Rebekah loved Jacob
And that was the reason they couldn't make up!

Eve

Eve be wary
Eve be wise
Or you'll have a bad surprise
Eve was foolish
Eve was bad
Eve made all the people sad
You be wary
You be wise
Or you'll have a bad surprise
If you're foolish
If you're bad
You'll make all the people sad

Adam

Adam, first man, met his God
A-walkin' in the garden
Said Adam first man to his God,
"Let me be your warden."

"Great," said God to Adam first man
A-walkin' in the garden
"You can name the animals
That dwell in Eden's garden.

Ballad of Ninevah

Sail, ship, sail
Jonah's in the whale
Soaky, chokey, pokey, blokey
Seaweed makes me pale

Pray, Jonah, pray
Go the other way
Soaky, chokey, pokey, blokey
Seaweed makes me grey

Cough, whale, cough
Jonah, now you're off.
Soaky, chokey, pokey, blokey
Seaweed makes me cough

Off to wicked city
Poor Ninevah pity
Reachy, preachy, eachy, teachy
Don your sackcloth gritty

Repent, people repent
Or brimstone will be sent
Reachy, preachy, eachy, teachy
Sackcloth will be rent

God took care
The people for to spare
Reachy, preachy, eachy, teachy
Sackcloth now is rare

Glossary

AMBS: Associated (or Anabaptist) Mennonite Seminary

CMC: Conservative Mennonite Conference

CPE: Clinical Pastoral Education

CPS: Civilian Public Service

EMM: Eastern Mennonite Missions

GMF: Global Missions Fellowship of Mennonite World Conference

IMA: International Missions Association

LMC: Lancaster Mennonite Conference

LMS: Lancaster Mennonite School

MCC: Mennonite Central Committee

MCF: Mechanicsburg Christian Fellowship

MKC: Meserete Kristos Church (Ethiopia)

MPC: Mennonite Partners in China

PIPKA: Mennonite mission agency of GKMI Indonesia

RBC: Rosedale Bible College

RBM: Regions Beyond Ministry

RMM: Rosedale Mennonite Mission

RI: Rosedale International

SIM: Sudan Interior Mission

VS: Voluntary Service

WMI: World Missions Institute

YES: Youth Evangelism Service

www.ingramcontent.com/pod-product-compliance
Lightning Source LLC
Chambersburg PA
CBHW060409130626
46555CB00005B/2015